THE MAJOR ORDEALS
OF THE MIND

HENRI MICHAUX

The Major Ordeals of the Mind

and the countless minor ones

Translated by Richard Howard

A Helen and Kurt Wolff Book

Harcourt Brace Jovanovich, Inc.

New York

Copyright © 1966 Éditions Gallimard
English translation copyright © 1974
by Harcourt Brace Jovanovich, Inc.

All rights reserved. No part of this publication may
be reproduced or transmitted in any form or by any means,
electronic or mechanical, including photocopy, recording,
or any information storage and retrieval system,
without permission in writing from the publisher.

Printed in the United States of America

Library of Congress Cataloging in Publication Data

Michaux, Henri, 1899–
　The major ordeals of the mind, and the countless minor
ones.

　"A Helen and Kurt Wolff book."
　Translation of Les grandes épreuves de l'esprit et
les innombrables petites.
　Autobiographical.
　1. Michaux, Henri, 1899–　　2　Drug abuse—Personal
narratives. I. Title. [DNLM: 1. Drug abuse—
Personal narratives. WM270 M622g 1974]
PQ2625.I2Z5213　　848'.9'1207 [B]　　73-16237
ISBN 0-15-155720-9
ISBN 0-15-655250-7 (pbk.)

First edition
A B C D E F G H I J

CONTENTS

I. THE MARVELOUS NORMAL   1
    A. Disorientations   3
    B. What Is "Coming to Oneself"?   8

II. IN DIFFICULTY, BUT WHAT DIFFICULTY?   25

III.   43
    A. Inmost, Continuous Alienations   45
    B. Further Alienating Transitions   62

IV. THE PRESENCES WHICH SHOULD NOT BE THERE   71

V. DIVESTMENT THROUGH SPACE   89

VI. RAVAGED SELF-CONSCIOUSNESS   103

*VII. THE NEED TO OVERLOAD AND
TO DE-SIMPLIFY* 121

VIII. EXPERIMENTAL ALIENATIONS 131
  A. 133
  B. The Unexplained Immensity 146

IX. THE FOUR WORLDS 153

  Comments 168

I. THE MARVELOUS NORMAL

A. Disorientations

I want to lift the veil from the "normal," the unrecognized, unsuspected, incredible, enormous normal. The abnormal first acquainted me with it, disclosing to me the prodigious number of operations which the most ordinary of men performs, casually, unconcerned, as routine work, interested only in the outcome and not in the mechanisms, however marvelous, far more wonderful than the ideas he sets such store by, which are often so commonplace, mediocre, unworthy of the matchless instrument that reveals and plies them. I want to lift the veil from the complex mechanisms which make man, first and foremost, an operator.

One day, at the movies, after taking hashish, a strange, unfamiliar, unpleasant sense of deficiency mounted within me, soon becoming intolerable. In spite of all my efforts, I could not tell what city I might be in. This persistent lack of orientation ultimately got the better of my enjoyment and my patience, and I left the theater. Outside was the same old Paris, the same old Left Bank. Should I go back to the theater? I wavered, decided against it. To face all over again that uncharted darkness was too much for me. True, I had recaptured a sense of place. Some sense of place. At moments, a complete sense of place; but over and over again, erratically, in ten or a hundred different ways, I kept losing track of it. What was happening? I was *disoriented*. Meaning what? Disjointedly disoriented by countless disorientations, incessant, incessantly different, unpredictable; dismayed by discontinuities in orientation. I had to admit it: from birth, I had spent most of my life orienting myself.

Vigilant of necessity, unremittingly struck by the flashings, the shocks, the calls which signal, alert, warn on all sides, I had—like any man alive—been made to take bearings, second by second to take, to retake my bearings, a ship navigating the strange, the alien, sea, held to these indispensable operations in order to remain aware of an ever-changing situation.

Such is the crucial, the preferential concern of the intelligence—not reading, study, examinations. I could not get over it. A sleeper, a dreamer, I had unwittingly been a prodigy of vigilance, of speed. Dawdling, lazy, I had been nonetheless diligent, and enterprising, and perceptive, and searching. As everyone is.[1] How can this be so?

Just as the stomach does not digest itself, just as it is essential that the stomach do no such thing, the mind is constructed in such a way that it cannot grasp itself, cannot directly, continuously grasp its own mechanism and action, having other matter to grasp.

Not until insidious derangement by a drug had brought this mechanism to a halt did I at last, quite late in life, realize experimentally so vital, almost omnipresent a function, whose incessant action had just ceased. This sudden

1. Every animal, in fact, though in a less co-ordinated way.

revelation of everyday unconsciousness was so confounding that I would never be able to forget it again; it gave me notice to seek it elsewhere, however omnipresent it might be, to the point where one might almost say that thinking is unconscious. This is probably true of ninety-nine per cent of thinking: a hundredth part of consciousness has to suffice.

Thinking, the micro-phenomenon in the fullest sense of the term, its numerous meshings, its many silent micro-operations of dislocation, of alignment, of parallelism, of displacement, of substitution (before achieving a macro-thought, a panoramic thought) escape consciousness and must escape it. They can be followed only exceptionally, under the microscope of a desperate attention, when the mind—monstrously excited, for example, from the effect of large doses of mescaline, its field of vision altered—sees its thoughts as particles appearing and disappearing at stupendous speeds. Then it grasps its own "graspings," a state altogether out of the ordinary, a unique spectacle, a windfall of which, however, distracted by other wonders and by newly discovered tastes, by mental processes of which he would previously have been incapable, the drug taker has little thought of taking advantage.

Yet this singular revelation is not of a kind readily to convince those to whom it is reported; despite and perhaps because of its seemingly excessive obviousness, which may appear suspect. Sometimes the ex-visionary himself, once he returns to normal after such intense awareness of "that" which leaves no more than quite imperceptible vestiges, no longer knows what to think.

Fortunately, this revelatory manifestation is not the only one. In quite different ways, in many ways, the drug catches out, discovers, unmasks mental operations, injecting consciousness where it had never been, and at the same time dislodging it from places where it had always been: a queer case of drawers that can function only alternately—some must be closed before others may open. The many operations which in the natural state escape detection then become detectable; I am here concerned to pursue them—after the fact. I intend to rediscover them, changed no doubt, but not altogether, since I am utilizing the same tool which cannot so vary with itself.

Conscious or not, they must surely be there, those micro-investigations, micro-manipulations, micro-stages, the very texture and fabric of the mind. I feel it as a kind of obligation to track them down, to overtake them. I can never, ever, adequately proclaim the modest, instrumental aspect of the mind, its workmanlike quality, having known it on the verge of breakdown, when it was abandoning me in areas which by means of other still alert areas I scrutinized as best I could, and abandoning me in yet other ways when, miraculously but dangerously active, it was carried away.

What I was able to do before (when I was normal), what I could no longer do afterwards (in the abnormal state), and what, back to normal again, I could do again; what, dozens and dozens of times over, I could do, could no longer do, or first had great ease and then extreme difficulty in doing—that is the investigation I am undertaking, imperfect, it is true, yet essential.

Aside from my own experience, I shall be drawing support from and establish continuous points of comparison with those who have known the mind in its grievous state and those who in a more general manner have had serious difficulties with it—difficulties of understanding.

Just as the body (its organs and functions) has been chiefly known and revealed not by the prowess of the strong but by the disorders of the weak, the sick, the infirm and injured (health being incommunicative and a source of that vastly mistaken impression that everything proceeds as a matter of course), it is the disturbances of the mind, its dysfunctions which shall be my informants. More than the all too excellent mental skills of the metaphysicians, it is the dementias, the backwardnesses, the deliriums, the ecstasies and agonies, the breakdowns in mental skills which are really suited to "reveal" us to ourselves.

. . . .

B. What Is "Coming to Oneself"?

What, among other things, is experienced by the drug taker when the effect of mescaline, LSD, or some other shock substance of the same type wears off and disappears.

He is restored to thought. Thought is restored to him.

Just now, repeatedly and for long stretches of time, conscious of nothing, of nothing but nothing, *tabula rasa* (not the *tabula rasa* of the philosophers, always potentially inscribed and in no way alarming, where simply—a rich man's luxury—it has been agreed not to set down anything except little by little, in a preordained sequence, and without any untidy fringes), a real blank blackboard, he was at a point where nothing has ever been seen returning, nothing, nothing at all, and not the slightest sign that anything ever might.

Now, without yet thinking of anything very specific, the moment of nothingness has passed, that is obvious, that is certain.

Consciousness includes consciousness of the magic wand

of re-consciousness, the confused yet confident impression of the proximity of thought, of the imminence of thought, of an abundance of thought soon within reach.

He no longer had it. He has it again.

The mental tide in which all thought is elaborated returns, has returned. He is going to have a thought. It cannot fail. . . . Here comes one, here's another. They flow in, resuming their interplay. The mind works again.

Just now, at other distressing, agonizing moments, his thought was dangling, as though outside the orbit of his brain, held in by who knows what, with something refractory or alien about it, out of reach, vague, noxious, like some poorly focused image, above all elusive, oscillating.

His head felt sometimes like a relay station between other heads, sometimes like a target aimed at by others, or even like a mechanism partly out of his control which had been teleprompted by outsiders—the real owners of it—and which they had caused to function and to think in their fashion. Whatever the explanation, however singular, however bewildering, the fact remains that he was no longer the master, anything but "in" on it—not even knowing where to "take it into his head" to go.

Finished! The hours of alien occupation are over. Now he is alone in his brain. A wonderful feeling. Inner enjoyment of rights, perhaps the inmost of all, so private as to be virtually identical with the "self," clinging inseparably to the living being, and whose absence is a basic, inexpressible, unremitting catastrophe. Singleness regained, what a windfall, a godsend! No one but himself in *his* self. Now his thought is in fact thought by him, and by him alone, to the exclusion of all others, any other. Without its being absolutely subservient, at least it is dealing with him, him first and foremost, him only, as its manipulator, as its operator.

Even if its origins can be traced back to others, he is rethinking it, refashioning it in his own way, without any outside interference distracting him. Or imposing its thought upon him.

The incapabilities of the insane (for it is unmistakably they, once the drug has subjugated him) are now his capabilities, his restored capabilities.

He can turn back, remember; orient himself in his memory, in his surroundings, in his future. He can think. He can stop thinking. He can start thinking again. He can repatriate his earlier thoughts. He can resist the incontinence of thought, he can oppose contradictory thoughts. He can follow thoughts as he pleases, adjust, readjust them, bring them within his control, co-ordinate them.

He can make conjectures, estimates that will stand up to tests, to criticism. He can evoke . . . calculate, manipulate figures, symbols.

He can, he can, he can. He can . . .

He has full powers. He has regained them. For that is what thinking amounts to—this, and much more; among other operations it consists in placing elements in the field of thought, in reaching yesterday's experience, for the impression of five minutes ago, of a year ago; it means being able to formulate and fix a thought, to keep it from escaping, from being independent, unresponsive to your mediations. It means keeping it clear from all preceding ones. It means being able, while listening or reading, to keep two subject matters, two sequences of thoughts, from coalescing, preventing not only their uncalled for entanglement, but the impregnation of the second by the first. It means keeping words, sentences, paragraphs, once they are recorded, at bay, resisting their attraction and allure in order to be able to proceed to what follows.

Far from being a powerless witness, one is more generally

enabled to face up. To resist here, to accept there. To be accessible at certain moments, and inaccessible at others.

To try, to try again, correct, improve, following a plan, a program.

HE IS EXERCISING CONTROL OVER THINKING, HIS OWN CONTROL.

All that was left to him had been analogical thinking (and even that intermittent only, and peculiarly "runaway") which took shape in him beyond his control, flashing free, independent, at extravagant speed. Now he has regained a constructive, co-ordinated kind of thought, which can examine its object freely from all sides, deliberate thought, thought in stages.

To arrive at such thinking is an athletic feat—you have to be in excellent shape. Or rather, as the sailor at the helm can guide and steer a ship of thirty thousand tons with one hand, provided he disposes of the power reserve of the auxiliary motor; it requires only minimal attention to utilize it, for maneuvering.

All this flows back to him too readily, all at once. This unique opportunity to perceive clearly by contrasting the effect of his restored incapabilities and his incapabilities of barely half an hour ago, incapabilities, moreover, which in many cases stemmed from superabundance; this opportunity which he must seize does not last, it is rare, extremely rare, soon he will be overrun by memories, by overwhelming experiences already registered, and toward which he is still nostalgically turning, under their spell, as it were.

Though he is in a state of exhaustion, of peaceful subsidence, of a "becalmed sea"[2] in which he would like to

2. Admirably described a century and a half ago by Humphry Davy, apropos of the terminal effect of the nitrous oxide he had just discovered.

remain, yet he must force himself to observe in detail what is happening to him. For as instructive as the drug state is the *after-drug state,* and especially what might be called the immediately-after-drug state.

Back among the powerful of this world, among the lords of mental health, all one with his new role, he soon turns renegade (this is a universal law), he forgets the paupers of the mind's powers (of pragmatic powers), the pauper he himself has momentarily been, the pauper's condition. No longer is he struck by how much strength is required in order to "execute" the least reflection, the simplest thought.

But this man of power is also a blind man. On more than one point, to recover one's self is to fall back into unconsciousness.

As, with mental health regained one changes consciousness, one also changes subconsciousness. Regrettably. The whole, subconsciousness and consciousness, is never within one's grasp at once. . . . The truths, the discoveries made only a moment before, sustained by experience but soon losing that support, are now so riddled by gaps, holes, loss of context that they might be considered of no more value than wild hypotheses.

For during that time there was more than paralysis and *tabula rasa.* Alternating with the blocks, there were periods of overactivity, of high stimulation and accelerated thinking—thinking detached from all practical use and freewheeling, as it were (and therefore inapplicable[3] to such mental operations as computation, strategy, grouping, reasoning, and memorizing).

3. LSD, at present the subject of experiment in the U.S. Army with a view to its possible use in chemical warfare, was chosen because of its power, in sufficiently strong doses, to inhibit all ability to calculate, scheme, and make decisions. Spread in the right places, the "miraculous" powder would disorient an entire headquarters and reduce it to helplessness.

What took place, though, was an extraordinary spectacle, a seething functioning, ineffectual and superhuman, which deserves frequent scrutiny, precisely because it is impossible to distinguish, within it, what is basic to the human being and what is abnormal.

What, then, a moment ago, became manifest to him with such clarity and self-evidence?

It is the *unique nature* of thinking, its life apart, its sudden birth, its disengagement, its independence which keeps it way above language, with which it conjoins only rarely, momentarily, provisionally, uncomfortably. At best, it precedes language, merges with it for an instant only to leap forward again, to leap aside, apart,[4] returning for new departure, elusive, free, never for long mingled with anything verbal or gestural or emotional, never truly immersed or dissolved within it. Yet never soft or vague either, as incapable of softness as electricity.

Thinking (as he saw it then, a new *Gegenstand*, with all the certainty one has before an object) has no fluidity. No fluidity whatever. It is language which has fluidity, which creates that regular, convenient, familiar trickle that one calls and refers to under the name of thought, which introduces us to thought . . . quite imprecisely.[5]

Everything in thought is somehow molecular. Tiny particles that appear and disappear. Particles in perpetual associations, dissociations, reassociations, swifter than swift, almost instantaneous. For thought is abrupt. Downstage, the devil leaping out of his lair, jack-in-the-box.

4. For one digression (or one parenthesis) of speech, there will be incidentals and side leaps of thought.
5. Speech "preserves" and the written word remains . . . but thought has moved on, outdistancing the "interim report." Each man who periodically casts anchor in language does so to keep in touch with his fellow men . . . and then sets out again alone in the world of his mind.

A schema appears, disappears, reappears with a slight modification, but still distinct, disappears again, reappears with a new slight or great but always pronounced change.

Nothing is vague. No more vague than in the electronic or chemical actions or operations in which the bodies can only obey, quite strictly, the specific valences of their atoms.

That is what he had witnessed a short time ago. Was it real? Is it still real? Or was it a kind of shadow, an overlay, a representation which doubled the true phenomenon of ideation, being not its true image but only the reinforcement, the emphasized translation of one of its epiphenomena, which is normally unperceived, and rendered visible at this moment?

This may well be, for there is, in these exceptional moments, a very strong visualizing and representational tendency.

Thinking, if it is in fact the way he saw it then, in any case involved precise location and displacement. The "mental object," or schema, or thought accompanied by a schema (something like the molecular schemas of stereo-chemistry), but constantly in a state of reorganization (a reflection is a reorganization), gave way to a slightly different configuration, which gave way to a second one, which gave way to a third, precise though always different, which gave way to a fourth, to a fifth, to a sixth, to a seventh, to a tenth, to an eleventh, to a twelfth, etc., to a twentieth, to a hundredth, in an abundance similar to the wastefulness of nature in reproduction of plants, of fish, or of insects. And so, dazed by the nondefinitive character of these endless repetitions, and by the impossibility of pausing over any one of them, one could, one can, exhausted as one is, consider all this as confusion; yet not for an instant, not at any point, has there been confusion: confusion is impossible. Vagueness is confined to the impression of discomfort which accompanies the difficult labor of arrangements, of patterns. For there are always patterns. A profusion of patterns. To reflect is to be in mid-pattern. Here one realizes the need for strength (or will power), in order to be able to act, to orient oneself, to recall, to fix. One becomes aware of the splendid mechanism by which it is possible, thanks to a swift exploratory operation, to continue projecting the pattern on the screen of consciousness, over and over again, improving it with every new projection, until after perhaps two hundred, or a thousand attempts, a provisionally satisfying state—or a definitive and beguiling one—is achieved. From dozens or hundreds of such combinations, of attempted integrations hitherto virtually or altogether imperceptible, a thought finally emerges, a conclusion sufficiently blunt and satisfying to be received (as much as perceived) and which the long eclipse of active intermediary states, of subthoughts and mental subformations, has made possible. For however illuminating an idea may be, it always is part of a pattern, creates itself, organizes itself by pattern, the pattern of gropings and uncertainties or of inexplicable certainties or of inexplicable certitudes, partial or total, by attraction of affinities or opposites, a pattern which at times, in his recent state, he was unable to achieve, having lost all authority, or a pattern which was created in and of itself, without him, astounding and visible, or which in a mental failure, a particular "fading," gradually came to a halt, or, for no discernible reason, extended playfully, unable to contain itself, the way a pianist runs up and down his scales. And reality, even external reality, seemed to have become unreal, factitious, false, unrecognizable. (Reality is the result of authority. The mythomaniac, the dreamer, even at their worst, possess authority without knowing it.)

He saw what was even more singular.

He noticed one of those phenomena one then wants to eliminate from memory, behaving as though one had not noticed, so disconcerting do they seem at first glance, and apparently entering into no synthesis, and unsusceptible of any valid explanation.

Yet these are phenomena which must not hastily be declared aberrant and anomalous.

For instance, the spectacle of oppositional thought.
For instance, the spectacle of repetitive thought.

The two being, at such moments, ungovernable, and nonsignifying, useless—and prodigious.

Just as the images then often appear paired, according to a rigorous, elementary, exaggerated, spontaneous, almost mechanical, and insanely repeated symmetry,[6] the thoughts came in pairs, one provoking the other, one invoking the other (either similar or analogous, or antagonistic). Strange pairs they are, each thought with its contrary, the yes with the no, the pro with the contra, affirmation with negation, and if it were not too long, thesis with its antithesis, bent with its counterbent or countertaste, evident effects of a doubtless normal function which maintains thought under tension, but at this moment, incredibly exaggerated and multiplied, distressing and useless, distracting and driving to perpetual indecision, a phenomenon of irreconcilable

6. Corresponding to certain mediumistic drawings. Repetition is also (as Dr. Koupernik informs me), a constructive learning factor in the child. A habit of which some traces remain.

16

contradiction which endlessly returns to the charge, incessantly traumatizing . . . permitting us to understand the ravages it can make in a schizophrenic, as it sets up an insoluble ambivalence, expression of the hell of an irreducible antagonism, experienced with no chance of ever escaping from it, either by progressing beyond it or by a final affirmation.

The opposition of antithetic thought, which keeps the primary thought in check, may also be seen in precipitate alternations which seem to derive from a current or from a spasmodic phenomenon rather than from reasoning. All the same one should not forget that they are a topic of development (by contrast) and constitute a natural treatment of the idea. These maddening alternations could therefore be efforts at composition—rudimentary, desperate, botched, and vainly rebegun, with what little in the subject remains of directing strength. The same is true of the equally present repetition (another primordial topic), here, as was to be expected, exaggerated, mechanical too, turning thought, which launches into futile enumerations, into an explosive quantum whose discharges can only be passively observed until its exhaustion. Unable to develop, thinking is discharged in useless repetitions.

Thus or otherwise, it becomes obvious, even spectacularly so, that a thought, even of discouragement, is energy, is the appearance of a certain quantity of energy which takes place, which takes successive places, which precipitately effects its rapid formations, rapid indeed until after many ricochets it comes to a halt, drained, exhausted, its life completed.

In all these ways, thought shows a striking and almost electrical discontinuity (instead of the continuity and interlocking that constitutes the nature and tendency of the sentence), and at these moments[7] at least it is not for nothing that thought is linked to neurons, which discharge periodically.

Now that it is almost over, now that the crises of repetition, the maddening enumerations and theses-antitheses have come to an end, now that the ungovernable can be governed, now that everything abates, and now that, further, he can even deliberately reinforce that abatement, now that it is possible for him to reason[8] clearly once again, to judge, to decide, to conclude, and now that thinking, instead of explosions, of violent oppositions and momentary illuminations, is rather to proceed to discreet accommodations, he also returns to the speech-thought adjustment, a more comfortable one. But like someone who, having made a journey abroad, no longer retains his national naïveté, is no longer altogether at home, has taken his distance—and kept it.

The old coupling of thought and speech is now forming again before his eyes. Speech obliges thought to follow its own uneventful path. Thought must join the procession of words, must put on the garment of words, must enter the inscription of words, must attach, alter, think itself by way of words. A fall[9] into verbalization. Once it has befallen, there is a certain comfort.

7. Yet simultaneously—as an unexpected stage, an incredible detachment—there occurs an awareness of the transcendent, of an absolute transcendence, utterly opposed to all that is superficial or accidental. A conversion to ESSENCE, to the Absolute, has been made.
8. To pursue an argument, to manage to group its elements simultaneously or successively, to keep track of them, to vary them, change them, modify them, to maintain enough mastery to put an end to arguments, in order to judge, in order to decide, what a marvel! Previously he had had no idea of it, of all that it presupposes!
9. And experienced as such.

It is also a reconquest, and a very flexible one.

He feels at ease in words, in sentences. In step with them at their pace.

A short time ago, he was often at a loss where to look for them, they were lost, alien, inaccessible, irrecoverable, outside the mind's field, or else they fell upon him in whirlpools, or rather passed before him in rushing parades, so fast he had no time to grasp one of them. Or if he managed to, they turned out to be meager, oddly enough always inadequate somehow, unsuitable, unusable as such. Silly, most of all. He stumbled over them to no avail. He would have preferred others, sometimes managed to find them, or rather it was they which spontaneously found him; invented, evocative clusters, yet unwieldy, bunched together anyhow instead of built, organized. Language seemed a huge pretentious clumsy machine which merely blurred all distinctions, and moreover escaped his grasp in a growing disqualification, in indifference.

To the point where he was tempted to enclose himself within an absolute silence.[10]

In this state, in fact, it is a sign of intelligence to drop words, and of stupidity to cling to them (thereby missing a possibility of transcendence).

Now the words come, come in handy, he rediscovers them, finds them satisfying. He finds them supportive. He takes pleasure in using them, following them, employing conjugations, connections, analogies, enumerations.

Language serves him, now that he has changed mental gears—returning to a pedestrian's speed, a gleaner's speed, a speed of retention, of reading, of computation, of scrutiny, memory, study.

---

10. A state familiar to many of those who take mescaline, and to schizophrenics who take nothing. In this singular state one refuses to speak; speaking is experienced as a profanation.

Once again he joins the word to the concept. He finds it natural that they should be joined, that they should remain so.

He has a social thought which can be communicated (without excessive loss). He did not have it before—he had been playing truant, a fated, obligatory truancy.

With a fruitful slowness, a slowness which permits a tremendous synchronization, he advances on and by words, accepting their help with a hope of getting on. He follows the sentence, not only following and accompanying it, but on his way to meet meaning.

Now the pragmatic returns, the useful, the adapted, the harmonious; the ego returns, with its limits, its authority, its annexationism, its possessiveness, its grasping, its delight in imposing, in amalgamating, in forcing at all costs. And it all seems natural!

Yet there is a danger here—more than one!

A danger of the excessive preference shown to communicable, demonstrable, detachable, useful thought, with the value of reciprocity, to the detriment of thought in depth, pursuing depth. A danger of its too-constant socialization.

A danger principally of excessive mastery, of excessive use of the directing power of thought which constitutes the particular stupidity of the "great scholarly minds," which no longer know anything but directed thinking (voluntary, objective, calculating) and knowledge, failing to leave the intelligence *at liberty*, to remain in touch with the unconscious, the unknown, the mystery.

And what about this slowness of his? On what does it rest? Can there really be such a thing as slowness?

He cannot believe it. He has seen enough to suspect the worst slowness of speed, and the worst passivities of countless interferences and manipulations.

Even daydreaming is now no longer a matter of vagueness. It must be something altogether different, something intensely active.

If, for the true dreamer, dreaming is to regain his freedom, for most people—preoccupation continuing its structuring—it is to shift the focus of their attention in all directions (forward, by plans and projects—backward, by memorization). Backward, let us say. Once again everything passes by at a very, very, very great speed (too great to become conscious of it), and it is only at a moment of surprise, when in the series rushing past him something appears that jars, that calls forth a sudden denial, or shame, or regret, or correction[11]—it is then that, in the recapitulation, there is a sudden start, and consciousness.

Otherwise the reversals of direction are unconscious. Moreover, if memories were not both fantastically rapid and almost unperceived, we would spend all our lives in them.

Speed! Can we forgo extreme speed? Can the mind forgo it? For those who have experienced the unforgettable accelerated tempo of mescaline, speed invariably remains *the* problem, doubtless the key to many others, a problem whose precious elements, discerned at these unique moments, are all the more difficult to explain and demonstrate to listeners the more deeply they have astounded the experimenters.

What do they say, for example? That they lived a century in a quarter of an hour. Why a century, why not ten hours or the length of a day? But that is not what they say—they say "a century."

Some will even say that this speed has no relation to

11. In Gestalt-psychology experiments, it has been shown that we recall uncompleted actions better than completed ones. Perhaps slips and errors, misplaced objects, irritating oversights, return to memory in the manner of incompleted actions, that is —in order to be complete and satisfying and forgettable—deficient in a new operation.

normal mental speed, or even that they are talking about a time outside of time.

Questioned about the number of impressions per second (or of images, or of thoughts) experienced by them, persons returning from the speed of mescaline speak of an acceleration of a hundred or two hundred times, or even of five hundred times that of normal speed.[12]

But what is normal speed? How much information and integration can normally pass into the brain, from one second to the next?

Certain birds grasp, distinguish, up to seven hundred sounds a second and yet do not fail for a second to register colors, heat, light, shapes, movements of objects and of the air, or interrupt the appraisal of the data which serve for their balance, their subsistence, and their knowledge of the environment. Are man's mental signal systems so much poorer? It is not easy to decide with any degree of certainty.

Too many "touches" go underground, without making an impression.

A normal man is as much a being who absorbs as a being who forgets, who forgets many things and especially and immediately a hundred or a thousand impressions per second he has no need of keeping in mind.

The drug, let us remember, indicates, *reveals* more than it creates.

Intensity increases along with speed, an intensity reveal-

---

12. And what if it were twenty times? Or even only six times? Would that not be enough to be overwhelmed, to have (mistakenly) the feeling of a fantastic speed? In my own case, I have had the experience of seeing a whole film projected in a few seconds. Apparently complete. But was it really? With all its details? Doubtless with only the details that mattered to me, that counted for me, reduced then to essentials, perhaps to little enough, and which then could go fast. . . .

ing and emphasizing the speed already there, a speed now seen as much more considerable than previously supposed, an intensity which brings to perception the images (and micro-impulses) otherwise imperceptible, vague, and remote. The drug makes the subject conscious of many other transitions and also of desires, which become sudden, violent, lightninglike impulsions.

Not everyone, perhaps, is always so far from the speed.[13] If only such people could be aware of it. Calmly, words, sentences pass over abysses of speed. Let us not be fooled by them.

Man is a slow being, who is possible only as a result of fantastic speeds. His intelligence would have long since divined this, if it were not the very operation of intelligence.

. . . .

During his study, observations based on the normal state have seemed to the author disqualified from figuring in the present text.

On the other hand, pieces of information he expected to gather from accounts of states of near starvation or near death have been less fruitful, more scattered and difficult to find than he had supposed.

Once again, therefore, states of artificially induced anomaly will constitute the object of the following observations.

13. In certain emotions, in shock, falls, drowning, we see part of our lives pass before our eyes at tremendous speeds. Certain "lightning calculators" can complete computations in four or five seconds which take good mathematicians four or five hours to perform, and which represent thousands of operations. These prodigy arithmeticians are in other respects not at all remarkable. They are not geniuses, nor are they, on the other hand, pathological; they are ordinary men and women. By what dissociation, by what disconnection do they manage to take advantage of the real mental speed, to enter into a direct relation with it?

Sometimes these will be slight derangements, on the borderline of the normal, examined in the light of more serious states previously gone through, sometimes more serious states in the light of less serious states that are more readily, more accurately observable....

II. IN DIFFICULTY, BUT WHAT DIFFICULTY?

"I will tell. I wanted to tell, bringing in what went before, then out of growing incapacity because struck from a certain deflected angle or say I stop in my amazement expelled my mind an archipelago on the spot I continue correcting that is the difficulty correcting transforming jellyfish in stages the greatest encompassing attention waves which do not converge if someone astute enough and detached from first to last could realize . . . I encompass it all if what is before me a moment at least a place these divaricating sites, pinch, and now having experienced it, twenty and twenty, no not one . . ."

And so on.

After a pause I continue writing and the words return, regularly, as though dripping from a faucet, the drops reluctant to fall, but the words keep coming, though I realize that what lands on the sheet of paper is not, cannot be what I had intended, I struggle to correct, to get back on the track, but my efforts are like those a roadworker would make, trying to turn over the pavingstones with nothing more than a lark's feather in the way of tools.

Yet I continue to write, to add words, blindly aiming at the astonishing phenomenon which was the one thing worth getting down, while fragments of new sentences arise, deflect and repulse me, each in its own way. Almost placidly, although with each new spurt of syllables I am further delayed, further removed, I go on writing, mindful that it is with a view toward a highly unusual description that I have begun to write. I continue, though the subject of my writing is no longer in view, does not return, and it is clear, becoming clearer with each scrap of sentence, that I am invariably wide of the mark. Calmly I continue, emitting imperfect words which are only an approximation, a vague or quite inadequate approximation; but it seems I believe, since

At the start, after a busy day, I was feeling somewhat tired and unfocused, when the moment came to take the prepared substance[1] I had decided to try. Then I must have dozed off. Waking, still sluggish, feeling nothing out of the ordinary, I stretch, rub my eyes, when all of a sudden[2] . . . the bookcase moves, the shelves ripple. Amazing! An invisible power seems to be stirring them from end to end, as if they were pliable, soft.

So I am no longer in my normal state. I pick up a pencil and pad, determined to describe the extraordinary spectacle, which soon comes to an end.

Words come. Words. Not the words I want. Not properly linked. Not in the right order. Forming only a fragment of the sentence I am searching for, scraps, pieces. Here is what appeared on the page:

1. Suffice it to say that it affords hallucinations to those open to receive them, and meets resistance with discomfort.
2. Doubtless the phenomenon was released when I mechanically rubbed my eyes, but it continued entirely on its own, quite differently, once the spectacle had been initiated.

somehow these twenty or thirty scraps of words are links forming a trace to the "event," that eventually they or those still to come will attach me to it openly, and lead me back to the desired memory. It exists, I know that, I feel it. Strange how it vanished . . . and so easily. While I was looking for a pencil, it was simply wiped out. A moment later, it might still have come back to me . . . This was not a foolish hope. Meanwhile a thought had occurred to me, filling the void of my expectation. Before I reacted, that thought too had vanished. The first having disappeared, I wanted to write down the second, because of the connection it must surely have had with the first, that first one connected with the "event," but in trying to express it clearly I fell behind, and now a third thought was appearing, and I was about to write it down (it actually dealt with the difficulty of such notation, but from another angle) and the word "deflected" appeared, probably not the right word; the same with the word "distracted," of which, hesitating, I had time to write only the syllable "dis," when a new thought occurred to me, which I didn't want to let pass without writing it down, yet as with its predecessors I managed to find only two words out of the six or seven which would have been necessary to capture it; meanwhile the next thought was already there, summoning me, of which I got down a word or two (it wasn't only the leakage of ideas, actually there were some which were quite slow, but their transcription was so slow!), so that I barely made a dent with this approximate, belated inadequacy of words resulting from the preceding notion and mingling with the next, for better or worse, helter-skelter, "surfacing" by themselves, without the idea . . .

Overlappings, repetitions (repetition here means the attempt to regain control), dislocations, juxtaposed leavings of disparate scraps, my central preoccupation pushing on among them as best it could, awkward, unintelligible—that is what the long, almost uninterrupted sentence was, that and so much else—an accumulation of various debris, relating to various thoughts arrested in mid-phrase, crisscrossing, and too complicated to try to correct then and there

I kept drifting. In the same way a swimmer, carried away by a powerful crosscurrent, will sometimes, despite his regular strokes, find himself swept far from the shore to be reached. But not only was I moving away from the shore, I was losing sight of it, glimpsing another one from which, equally, something was sweeping me away, until—how intensely I was aware of this!—I lost sight of it too; another was appearing, I wanted to head for it, yet my very movements were carrying me in the wrong direction, I was losing sight of it; a fourth appeared, which I was leaving behind at the very moment I was trying to approach it, and there were four, five shores, ten, twelve shores, who knows how many shores from which I was successively repulsed.

But my sentence which was my own kind of swimming persisted, since I was obscurely convinced that by keeping contact, however defective, with what was going through my mind, though very little through my writing, I would sooner or later rediscover the memory from which I remained inexplicably cut off.

And then, in the midst of this Sisyphean task, without any warning, returns, returned the recollection of the memorable episode:

"From front to back, from back to front, the rows of books on my library shelves, undulating, advanced and retreated in ample dancelike accordion movements." That was it, that was what I had seen and had wanted so desperately to write down, that flow of such independent amplitude, that superb, majestic undulation which, I discover from my watch, made its appearance about fifteen minutes ago. A quarter of an hour to rediscover so astonishing a phenomenon! Which I note down in three, four words, to enable me, later on, to recall the whole thing (I hope), for now it is over, a memory vanished into the darkness. A thought has come to me, has launched me. I am back in the current. Back with my problem, which is: "What does all this mean? What is happening to me? What is impeding me?"

How stupid it all is! I seem to be writing not in order to get closer to what is to be said, but in order to get away from it. Writing with the greatest application,[3] I invariably end up wide of the mark.

The speed, noticeably increased, is not yet extreme. The phenomenon is elsewhere. It lies in the fact that the scraps of the sentence do not converge, I cannot force them to do so, words are like cliff faces, cliff units which do not interact, do not truly join. Why? Because in dealing with words, joining is always joining with a view to something (an idea, a need) which prevails over the others, which will serve the others, or which the others will serve. And there is always someone who makes them join, makes them serve, subordinating one to the next, integrating them with a third, there is someone whom this pleases, who finds it appropriate, who

3. I should add that, fascinated by the strange impediment, I made no aesthetic effort whatever. Surprisingly, I was not aware of this at the time, and did not notice what, from this point of view, might be more or less interesting.

All I noticed was the absence of harmony. To this verbal disorder there corresponded, indeed, no sense in myself of the disordered.

is its author, or at least its arranger. This "someone," here, can no longer do this. He sees that what is called for is to inflect, to influence, to orient, to prepare, to justify, to introduce, etc., everything he was not aware of as entering into the simplest "statement" for it to hang together.

But someone who could do this, could introduce, bring together (for even to set up opposites is to unite, a kind of joining), shed light on the relations between ideas . . . that someone is missing. The elements remain isolated units.[4] The grammatical links, often incorrect moreover, must not mislead us. The profound links which create the authentic union are missing because administrative thinking, incessantly synthesizing and resynthesizing, is missing, thinking which in the course of writing considers the various possibilities of the sentence and *selects*.

Every thought, I realize, must, in relation to the sentence, be constantly *re* thought, *re* composed.

As for the "someone" here, all this is now beyond his means. Everything else follows from that. Unable to formulate, he is still less capable of reformulating. To correct is impossible. To restore interdependences, impossible. To change directions, impossible. At any rate it is a formidable undertaking which he must abandon long before he can succeed. Is this senseless? No one is more concerned with "sense" than he.

At the time of writing, the meaning is there for him, and also the meaning deflected by the wrong word, and the meaning which that word should have expressed, which, if it

4. Even the most involuntary, the freest thought or image, at the very brink of the unconscious, must, if it enters language, be put in its place (a place in relation to others). An infinitesimal, imperceptible, instinctive intervention places them, suffices to place them. This infinitesimal action, it seems to me, would still have been too much for me.

were corrected, could still be brought to perfect expression; but while he seeks the right turns of phrase, having sketched part of the sentence, or even finished this sketch, the meaning has vanished as though in a high wind or seems to be waiting out of reach, extremely attenuated, unusable. Another thought comes (another turning). Entirely absorbed by the meaning of this one, he no longer clings to the others. Their connection, glimpsed for a moment, is taken from him. Reasoning too becomes an embarrassing, hampering business,[5] with stages missing, with fantastic, or merely astonishing, suspect results. He must frequently abandon them, or abandon[6] following them to their conclusion, in order not to be utterly confused.[7]

Enough about what did not work. What did not work was the other side of what did, what worked amazingly, grandly, differently.

5. In part because of the disappearance or virtual disappearance of the successive intermediary propositions.

6. As is remarked by Mary Coate in *Beyond All Reason: A Personal Experience of Madness,* preposterous, extravagant, false ideas constantly occur to the mind. Impressions, associations constantly lead down the path of the fantastic. The fantastic is all that is most natural, but . . . it is no help. The sick man is the man who cannot reject such impressions and associations. The mentally healthy man is a perpetual corrector of fantastic impressions. The poet at times attempts to celebrate them.

7. Anyone who, under the effect of a neurodysleptic, wants to observe in himself the operation known as reasoning, will realize early how much he has altered from this point of view, and why. No longer seeing the chain of implications and not readily sustaining their totality, he is led to *desert* reasoning, to neglect it, as uncertain (nothing being demonstrable any longer), or to reason falsely. At such times he will notice how easily this is accepted, without any sense of disturbance—a discovery that may shed light on the case of those blocked minds known as mental defectives.

No thought was ordinary henceforth. Every thought became pervasive, and though quickly curtailed, prevailed nonetheless. Each one offered me its presence, its unique presence. It bestowed that presence upon me. In a few seconds' "exposure" it showed me its singularity, its otherness. As if it were a substance, a *metasubstance*.

Without being in a contemplative state (attempted in other cases, and which my present preoccupation, my problem, would have sufficed to prevent), I fulfilled one of its conditions, but reluctantly, a workman who keeps thinking about his lost tool. I realized this once more: unlike the contemplative man, the thinking man treats ideas unceremoniously. He relates them, conflates them, translates them, hunts them down, picks them up, makes transfers, modifications, definitions. How far I was from that kind of workman!

I write less and less. Ideas without taking sides.

Unable to direct my thoughts, my presence in my thoughts preoccupies me. I watch myself having a thought. This spectacle overwhelms me, delights me, satisfies me.

This byway of thought, which our presence in it represents (habitually neglected in our preoccupation with the significance of thought, which is the only thing that matters to the active man), shows itself, singles itself out, makes a great impression, dismissing the rest as the perfume of a powerfully scented flower dismisses, overwhelms the investigation of botanical characteristics one had intended to undertake.

In this fashion I spent a rare interval of time which had no place in ordinary time. Occasionally I received astonishing confirmation of this. Letting my gaze stray to the window, as I do quite mechanically many times throughout the day and as I surely must have done only a short while ago, I hear myself say (mentally, yet quite loudly): "Ah! Leaves, how long since I've seen you."

And that is actually my impression, as though I were returning from a journey with a past filled with things.

Yet nothing happened except thoughts, and for a very brief period only, but thoughts like places, rooms, squares where I might have been, so that, though virtually none are remembered clearly, I kept some impression of them, such as one keeps of a day in the country, not because of a multiplicity which has not existed, but by the emotion of what one has experienced. At my window, at the sight of the linden tree, of the broad leaves of the paulownia, I felt like a returning exile, an emigrant restored from thoughts in which—entirely passive—I had been transplanted.

From a certain moment onward (I had taken another dose of the substance), writing became increasingly difficult, then impossible.

Interruptions, reverberations, overlappings. Tornadoes in the abstract.

And all of a sudden I understand . . .

These ill-handled, badly matched words, especially those I was just writing, clumsy, erroneous, increasingly inaccurate, wrongly positioned words, and (fascinated as I was by what I wanted to avoid) sometimes conveying the contrary of what I meant, words to bridge the gap (but the gap remained)—suddenly it struck me that these flawed sentences, never reaching their goal for all their deviations, would have gained me if shown to any reader the status of a mentally defective, unconscious of his own derangement, a poor wretch who was out of his mind. Having become an imbecile in words, it is true that I no longer grasped the wholeness, the particular wholeness that is formed by idea and sentence, but I did grasp other wholenesses, wholenesses which the sentence, even had it been perfect, could not express, unaccustomed as it was to this kind of extraordinary phenomenon which the mind perceived without the capacity to take hold of it.

Achieving only nonsense, I should have passed for an idiot, cut off from the life of the mind, whereas on the contrary I was entirely mind, living only by the mind, interested solely in the mind and even separated from all that is not mind. Yet the ordinary observer of ideas, of run-of-the-mill, ordinary, and stupid ideas, provided he was capable of formulating them, would have judged me in this way.

Through my mind's eye there flashed letters of mental patients which I had been given to read, pathetic letters full of approximate or incorrect words, repetitions, letters of no use (to others) which despite obvious efforts failed to reveal, to determine, to focus on their subject, but circled around, or rather, although ceaselessly returning to it, drifted and veered some distance from their goal, without ever reaching it, deranged but not in the ordinary sense of the word, deranged from their trajectory, their forward course, deranged from their *range*, at full (and futile) intellectual speed, verbally stateless.

How clearly I saw them—and how I should have liked to speak in their name!

Laboriously yet vainly groping for clarity and intelligibility, bleak yet calm despite the complaints that were often their object, their inchoate, chaotic sentences repeated without managing to add to their message—I now saw these letters with new eyes. If ever, I kept telling myself, if ever I recover my capacities, I must write in their name.

Turning back to my own placidity at that moment when I might have seemed at least singularly *diminished*, while I felt actually restored—how else to put it?—to the very center of my being, I recalled certain patients afflicted with memory gaps, dyslexia, astereognosis with the loss of a number of skills of their body or of parts of their body, so that they seemed pathetic invalids. Yet (and this is what astonished me) when they were not being bothered with tests or embarrassed by the presence of relatives, they often showed a placid expression which conveyed a certain indifference and even ease. Of course they no longer had that memory which their observers stressed so much, but they did not feel themselves deficient in memory altogether (there are so many kinds of memory). After all, there are many kinds of knowledge.

Except at examination times, they maintained an impression of fulfillment. What is so necessary in social life becomes secondary when this confrontation with others no longer takes place. It is not the essence, does not diminish the sense of the essential. What the psychiatrist calls deficiencies corresponds but little to the deficiency experienced by the person who harbors it.

The essential, the thing without which one no longer has being, is something altogether different. These defectives (and also "normal" subjects during experiments "diminishing" certain faculties and functions, reducing them to virtually nothing, in whom specialists found many incapacities), provided they were left in peace, felt they lacked *nothing important,* their essence untouched, more evident even—stripped of functions which on other occasions related them more effectively to the outside world.

The essence: what remains when one no longer needs to lower oneself, to keep busy, to function, to become finite, specific, small.

I had understood. (Or so it seemed to me.) A considerable impression—stimulating, exhilarating. But whereas in habitual life, what exhilarates the mind also exhilarates the body and (at least to some degree) animates breathing, the heart, excites the glands, warms the chest, this remained in the realm of the mind.

Instead of entering into the life circuit, it remained in the mind, releasing there, by its pressure, a violent animation. A spectacle was released. It was as if by an inner vision I was suddenly brought into the presence of a vast sphere. With its two poles. Each of these poles, all tension, all energy, illuminated two comprehensions.

Two systems, two modes.

One pole had as its generating word (or tributary) "explication." The generating word of the other pole was "that's it."

Explication gathered up its own series.

That's it gathered up its own series. Gathered up, rallied, emitted, produced, expelled.

At tremendous speed, magnetically, the poles exchanged their messages like peacocks spreading their tails, opposing each other, opposing their advantages, their homologues.

In parallel movement, or rather diagonally and in the margin, perceptions kept appearing, significations drastically geared down, leading to remote, starting significations, at another depth, at depths relating to origins, to ranges of signification ever more remote, more concealed, a chaotic semantics of derivatives ever in derivation and out of range. Occasionally one pole was more active, then faded, lost strength, while the other, encroaching, flung out its weapons, or rather the elements of its system of syllables and explanations. During this time the opposing pole was more at rest, but at a strained, electric rest which did not last, soon again letting the two poles measure themselves against each other, almost on equal terms.

I myself seemed to have no active role—I followed.

Thus the pole *"that's it"* and the pole *"explication,"* blind to their fundamental identity, furiously flung their dissimilarities at each other, regardless of their being merely divergent resemblances, that gave them their tonus; all this in my presence, though I surely did not seem to be their originator nor the partisan of one or the other. I was amazed, overwhelmed. I watched. I was in the theater.

A baroque performance, perhaps not so far from normal mental action as we think. The extraordinary created from what is almost ordinary, but as an apparition. Were these not, visualized by surprise, those "fields of force created in the imagination by the proximity of two different images" referred to by one author,[8] except that here I was dealing with idea words and the tension of their opposition preceding a conclusion, and not resolvable before the various aspects have been explored.

So it appears that even resemblances, before being reconciled (not necessarily, not simply, in a synthesis), must show their antitheses, the dynamic pulsions of their opposition.

8. Juvet, in *Structures des nouvelles théories physiques*, a text I did not know at the time and which I have subsequently found quoted by Gaston Bachelard.

But these so subordinate words (uttered, it seemed likely, in my unconscious), then visualized, activated in this wild moment-movie—did they matter for intellection? Probably not. They were the wrong place to start from. Inevitable? Inevitable that the extreme internal tension should translate itself into immediate action, into commotion. In such cases, the baroque always prevails, and the "apropos" rather than the main cause, which, watching from a distance, concealed, though present, seems to prefer to become esoteric.

It was, in any case, one of these astonishing mental "asides," of little use for relations with others, being incommunicable; asides which doubtless fill the heads of so many "alienated" subjects. Raised to its maximum, toward the converse of inexpressible wonders and extravagances they cannot "render," this incommunicability is doubtless at the origin of the attitudes taken by many of them and the source of great suffering for schizophrenics; for more than other mentally afflicted, they feel, despite their deficiencies, far from inferior in intelligence compared with their uncomprehending attendants who have the advantage over them.

Next, images in my imagination began to stream past, intense, gratuitous (?), their mystery impenetrable. Fast, then faster, extraordinarily fast.

Whereas the first were merely peculiar but of natural shape, suddenly it was as if they had received a command: "Now change!" And the changes were not felicitous ones, not the kind that an interesting reworking would call for or at least justify.

During the rapid procession of these extremely unusual images, which now I felt the urgent need to start recording, at least mentally, at least partially, it became impossible to do so, categorically impossible. I realized this—they left no trace. As soon as one had passed, it had vanished into nothingness, leaving nothing behind it, neither in the two or ten seconds of "immediate" memory, nor during the tiniest fraction of a second; not even in the most attenuated state. There was no duration. It all streamed past me without my grasping it, without my being able to grasp it—in any manner. Neither I nor anything else "faced" a single one of the images. Absolute nonfixation. The more astounding it was, the more rigorously ineffable.

My interior vision, however distinct, was lacking in something: that much I realized.

Ordinarily, I always have (everyone has) a continuum which confronts the image, the idea, a continuum in whose presence these images[9] stream by and which, without necessarily entering into conflict with them, is tested, marked, in the fashion of an elastic band; it is ceaselessly modified, ceaselessly shapes itself, if only minutely, but the minute change counts, it is the "imprint." Band, current, resistance, or whatever (chemical substance, basis of ribonucleic acid molecules[10]), this elastic continuum, which normally underlies any alertness, was absent. It was not "marked" after the passage of these images. Nothing of what should have been marked was marked. Nothing was imprinted. That tensional X which perpetually confronts the image (and any perception) no longer existed. I perceived, and intensely, but the spot, once the image had passed, remained vacant.

Vision came. I did not single out any image. Nor could I interpolate anything, neither a reflection nor any other associated image. Because of the speed?[11] Not only that.

9. Or these perceptions.
10. Ribonucleic acid apparently "allows" individual memory.
11. Reciprocally, the absence of interreflection and of deliberation might cause the increase in the speed of passage, so that retention and adequate deceleration become impossible.

Because of lack of judgment, of participation.[12] The images passed unqualified. I registered no image whatsoever, knew at each moment that I registered nothing. There was no retention. There would be no recollection.

Thinking back on all this, everything had passed with something of the quality of a myth, of a fable, in which the most favored, the richest man in the world is, the next moment, the poorest, the most "deprived."

Water in a sieve. Undeserved gifts squandered in a second. Automatically! But is there such a thing as absolute waste, absolute loss? Perhaps someday, like those drunkards who after their bout have forgotten all that happened while they were drunk, but who, at their next bout, recover their memory and recognize the drinking companions whom, sober, they did not "place" . . .[13] In the huge organism that a human being is, there always remains a waking zone, which collects, which amasses, which has learned, which now knows,[14] which knows *differently*.

To regain that knowledge.

12. The operation of recollection is perhaps impossible if there is no participation (however unconscious) with a view to its use in the depths of successive integrations.

13. The same is true of epileptics left, it seems, without any mnesic trace after an attack, but who "occasionally recognize themselves from fit to fit, like certain dreamers from dream to dream," according to the expression of J. Delay.

14. Patients who, in a perfect "successive forgetting" (Dr. J. Barbizet, 1965), twenty times in the day, at two-minute intervals, forget the visit the doctor has just made, and even the injections and painful treatments, though their dreams and sometimes their actions prove that, unconsciously, they have remembered.

III.

A. Inmost, Continuous Alienations

Diffuse agitation.
Difficulty in thinking.
Thinking according to my previous tendency, the point of view I had . . . The point of view I am led to abandon. I am overwhelmed by a current to the point where my thoughts move with this hyperactive, torrential, rushing "something" which I feel flowing by, passages which force me . . . Aligned up above, they have become excessive. Ideas which only an hour ago I would certainly have considered as false and rejected, now suit me, and appear better adapted than the preceding ones, which become clumsy, empty, insipid.

In my state of strange, locally determined, insidious, cryptic hypertension, it is excess which best complements this immoderate condition deep within myself, this state which has been aroused, brought into motion. Ideas falsified by complementarity, by harmonization. Ideas which, beyond my intervention, no longer control themselves, *aspire to transgression.*

Of what? Of anything, of every rule in the book and of the primary one, namely, that a thought must accommodate itself to others, or else end up in utopia, error, absurdity.

My handwriting begins to ∼∿∿∿∿∿∿∿.

This is not a matter of some physically rousing, heartfelt or verbal excess, but of a violence which is purely, mentally excess.

False ideas. Cold ideas. Demented ideas.

Something else: I no longer manage to discern clearly when one idea is in effect opposed to another. I experience a tendency to consider them equals, whereas they must be quite different, sometimes the contrary of one another. Ideas are carried along in a certain movement which makes them move *equally*, here or at some other level than that of significations, and by a kind of mutual pulsation, of shared undulation, they are paired, paralleled (independent of my choice or desire) so that despite their differences, which henceforth become insignificant, they remain harnessed together—almost identical, in the same register. It goes far beyond this, occurs despite my not entirely discarded reason, and despite the reasons there would be for rejecting this pairing, this tendentious unification, this unjustified identification. Do I accept? Not always. Although quite muffled, and in the background, there subsists a certain reluctance to let myself be handled this way, an unwillingness to see my ideas reduced to an identity which I know, at least in some cases, cannot really exist and which is a kind of trick played on me, a trick to which I decide from time to time to put an end.

Here is how I go about it: an operation in two phases.

First, by beating a hasty retreat toward the moment of the first appearance of the ideas in question, that is, before they were "fraudulently" equalized. This retreat is irksome, uncomfortable, and I do not entirely achieve my intention, that is, I do not manage to see these ideas as distinctly in opposition as they used to seem to be. They continue to be part of something, something like a mechanism (and not like a larger idea which would encompass them both), so that I cannot clearly discern where their difference resides—a difference which in any case no longer matters to me, no longer needs to be considered.

It would take more—I would have to be able to examine them separately to be convinced that there is actually a difference, a notable difference. But how? The procession of equals, of equalized and equalizing ideas, continues and shows no signs of disintegration. Yet the moment has come to act. At this point I make a new, difficult effort, which costs me dear. I must see this difference, which surely exists. Then, with a kind of psychic release, the operation is effected and the effort receives its reward. I notice that there is actually a difference, but I do not succeed in *re-experiencing* it, only in noticing it thanks to this sudden increase of attention which nearly overwhelms me.

Soon after, while, the task performed, I relax, it seems that analogously the new-found truth, like a person, also relaxes, and returns to the error, to the fatal omnipresent error, to the excessive and the exorbitant, and my ideas, previously acknowledged as in opposition, return to a scandalous "forced" identity. I see them once again shifting to their false resemblance, now even enhanced, an identity which my will has only briefly been able to interrupt. Everything needs to be done again.[1]

---

1. This, surely, is what happens in alienation: one never has really done with things, and has to do them over and over again.

The alienated subject will agree to come around to certain ideas, but less than an hour later, sometimes two minutes later,

And now there appears a different attitude with regard to the word, the word as substance to peruse, to write, to outline. A word, of course, is written in several stages, in groups of two, three, four, five, or more letters; each individual has his own unalterable capacity, like his stride—his capacity of three, four, five letters at once.

This measurement, too, is part of a personality—his way of composing, that is, of decomposing words.

Both mentally and muscularly, my stride has changed. I encompass more letters, my reach is wider, I write more at one stretch without raising the pen, I realize in one glance what can be encompassed in a single stride. "That's nothing," it is easy enough to say. But is it? It is a human characteristic which permits identification; which permits identifying *oneself*. Before writing, each of us has his own way of envisaging the portion to be selected (each of us has his own means of "selection"), the number of letters to be written, the rhythm. Seeing these manifestations altered, I know that I am no longer the same. Another kind of man is revealed to me, and in me. A change that involves, there is no doubt about it, a larger scope, and a new assertion(?) "of character."

But soon the phenomenon, having become conscious and doubtless excessively observed, diminishes, thwarted, and abruptly ceases altogether, my handwriting returning to its usual form.

---

he is where he was before. He will have to be led away again, from his place in error, where, because of a compelling involvement, he again finds himself summoned by the error to which he is strangely bound and which serves as his actual inner solace.

A pity, I felt I was facing life differently. I had supposed that this change would last, at least for some time.

Leafing through an illustrated magazine, I am repeatedly attracted by what should be of no interest to me and never was before: an advertisement for fabrics.

What inexplicably attracts me here and ultimately holds all my attention, fascinates and keeps soliciting me anew, are, spread over a double page, which appears enormous, the stitches, the superabundant, parallel, innumerable stitches, all alike, equal, of a woolen sweater, reproduced in color (monochrome). The juxtaposition of innumerable equal stitches, equal and identical, finds an incredible analogy with something beyond counting in myself as well, something perpetual or perpetuating. I have no need of diversity. No room in myself for shapes and forms at this moment when they can cause only trouble, diminish me, oppose me, restrict me, frustrate my pleasure. No, absolutely, I shall not see until later, fleetingly and reluctantly, that this constitutes a sweater which I don't want, which would not suit me, and I return to the endless and as it were purposeless stitches whose utilitarian function attempts to limit. Down with forms, I have no heart for them, I want none of them. They are no longer of my company.

Everything that continues, that is without number, juxtaposed, repetitious—that is what I am concerned with and want to be concerned with. However modest its nature, it is sufficient if my mind circulates within it, feels reinforced—nourished, released by this theme and companion and immensity (yes!) and God knows what else beyond.

A certain optical pleasure as well? Yes, if it is understood that it proceeds with a limitless inundation and continuation. Does this move me also mentally as symbolic representation of the texture of the universe? Perhaps. Perhaps.

A kind of extraordinary tactile imagination, consisting of saturation, produced by an endless repetition of the similar . . . Perhaps that too.

Without entirely committing myself, without taking the leap, I am also more willing than ever before to enjoy the science of numbers, which up to now I always intensely and aggressively resisted. I might even understand their fascination now.

The way in which I now represent them to myself, notably the numbers in arithmetical progression, that quality of an inhuman advance, dangerous, not to be stopped, with dizzying consequences, warns me that something is happening in me which might leave traces, which might someday—who knows?—be the point of departure for some unexpected renewal . . .

The photograph of an unknown man in a magazine. Beyond the photograph, I am face to face with this man. We are together. Having just been together (I have put aside his photograph), he retreats into the past in a few seconds, as rapidly as he appeared before me, and is now far away. But in the thirty seconds of our being together, he had become an intimate of mine, closer to me than if we had spent a whole afternoon with each other. Now I am left embarrassed, feeling disgraced by such close commitment, like someone who remembers having had inadmissible intimacies. After only half a minute! I try to swallow my shame. Who was this person? In my already superseded notes, I find no description of him. An ordinary person, not my sort, vulgar, a squat, a butcher or salesman, the very prose of existence. A pyknic.

I want to pour myself a glass of water. Have I as much as turned my head? I give a violent start. On my right . . . an unaccountable presence. I did not expect to find something of such bulk there . . . But it is merely an object, an inanimate object!

In my present state, my first reaction is never to attribute an inanimate condition to anything; that is only my last reaction. Possessed by the animate, by the extreme, the infernal animate, all I can attribute to anything is the animate, that extreme animate whose excess maddens me, and which I am forced to project, which I will project over everything unexpected which comes into sight. An object is a presence, primarily presence, and from presence, what demented movement might not ensue?

Then, seeing that I am dealing with no more than a pitcher of water . . . Fine. Let it stay there! The knowledge according to which this presence, as pitcher, is harmless has not deserted me. But the emotion this shock has given me has not deserted me either.

I had gone into the kitchen. I return to the dining room. Now there is a girl there—a young girl, sitting upright in a chair, waiting.

It does not take long to correct the mistake. It is my raincoat that is on the chair, folded in a position which, it is true, has something of the natural grace of a slender young girl. Having forgotten something, I return to the kitchen and come back into the dining room. Having forgotten something else, I return once more, and come back, and each time I pass in front of the "occupied" chair, I forget I have already decided it was not a girl but a raincoat. It is a "girl" I keep passing back and forth in front of, and it is in a girl's presence that I do this and not that in the dining room. Obliged to leave the room once more in order to do something else I have forgotten, I should like not to see her there when I return, but she is still there, and this time it is my brother as an adolescent who in my own body, using my legs, passes in front of her!

I feel I have become entirely a thing. Disturbing, for what if instead of a girl sitting still, I were dealing with a powerful presence!

. . . .

Have I unwittingly irritated myself by my passivity?

Suddenly noticing a tiny living head on the table, I wring its neck, irresistibly impelled to do so. In no time, I tear and crush the head, which then turns into nothing but the remains of crumpled paper which had wrapped a package of biscuits. All that is left is a corrugated white paper and some tinfoil, torn . . . but which takes only a little while to come again to disturbing life. Odd, all the same, how I "handled" this creature. Very unexpected. Of course it was a biscuit wrapping, nothing more. I know that perfectly well. It was also a disturbing, annoying, deceptive being, capable of anything.

This backward look was of no help. An attitude to be transcended. Moreover, it is the future which distresses me. The positive phenomenon. I am no longer master of the situation. A familiar sign: when you can no longer prevent things, objects, parts of objects from becoming faces, people, beings; or from turning into busts or masks which lie in wait, which will come to life.

All of which disorients me. I need some refreshment. I select a tangerine from a basket of fruit, peel it clumsily with my fingers. Someone in the mirror that faces me is watching me. This is not possible—there is only a bare wall facing me. There is a mirror behind me, but it would not face me, even if I were to turn around.

The tendencies to become animate, living, increase on all sides.

The irregular pieces of tangerine skin on a plate have the capacity, I am convinced, of turning into a woman. I try not to think about looking at them. In front of me there is a sort of bum or vagrant. "A sort of"? Correct—a pre-being, an "about-to-be." I sense a reflection in the room, and I turn around toward the third peel, which this time I cannot keep from becoming a woman.

It is too much for me. I must get out, leave the premises. Walking, however, might be counterindicated. We shall see. The armchair near the door—there is a presence[2] in that armchair. I walk past it, and out the door.

I walk down the stairs. Then a long blank interval.

Where am I? The street begins with a cliff. I take a few steps more . . . A cliff in Paris? Without my knowing it? Someone must have told me and I paid no attention. Still, a cliff! I must check this later, make sure.

And in the same way, so many things I must think about, which I must endeavor to clarify . . .

From now on, I try, for clarity's sake, to formulate some questions mentally. I don't get very far. I hear someone, repeating my unspoken words, syllable by syllable, very fast.

Ridiculous holding me up to ridicule. Vexing.[3]

2. Every armchair is made in such a way that it evidently invites, suggests, summons its complement: a seated person. I cannot see or believe a chair to be empty. Is it actually occupied? It is no longer unoccupied.

3. The victim of this condition (a frequent phenomenon in many mental diseases) will tend to see it as a practical joke, since it closely resembles a sort (an intention) of mimicking, of echoing, and therefore, though quite secondarily, of *mocking*. He will

My gestures, some of my gestures, I see internally and experience them as followed, doubled by many tiny rapid internal miniaturized gestures—gestures, so to speak, of the second rank.

I feel hampered, greatly hampered.

Back at home I take some notes, and I notice that, instead of myself, a girl, with her own delicate hand, is writing down my remarks. Perhaps a more regular writing has led me into this illusion, because of the (remote!) resemblance the writing might have with the docile, impersonal script of certain young people. Or does my hand, seeming thinner and paler than usual, suggest a feminine hand to me?

I have just taken a tranquilizer, a Librium capsule. Why? Because my hallucinogen is quite disturbing, upsetting, and its action seems to be lasting a long time.

---

say, naïvely, that his words are being repeated in order to ape him, instead of exploring the automatic aspect of the phenomenon, which in its crudeness and inappropriateness rather ridicules the ape and the *aper*, since they never hit on a new idea, never achieve the truly ridiculous. But the victim of mental illness, subject as he is to prolonged discomforts, is particularly vulnerable to this disconcerting attack, recognizing its upsetting quality much more strongly than the crudeness of the "maneuver." Also, this cruel monotonous repetition is not always and above all not at once felt by those who suffer from it as a strategy of mocking; actually, it is as little "calculated" as the bouncing of a voice off an echoing wall.

The human tendency being to personify, I might have said, had I accepted the hypothesis of outside interference, that it was due to an effort of sabotage of a very low, primitive, robotlike order.

Still, if the phenomenon had persisted, my resistance—that resistance which is the alertness of my critical sense—would have given way.

But wouldn't violent effects be more interesting to observe? Surely they would. This is probably not one of my enterprising days. Cowardice? To cover up, I tell myself that first and foremost I want to observe; if I am overwhelmed, propelled out of my consciousness, everything would be lost. Also, this is an opportunity to learn whether this tranquilizer has an anti-drug effect.

Still, not much reason to be proud of myself right now. "Myself" is letting me down.

Tension increases. I hear some obscenities in Spanish or in Portuguese.

Bad now.

Not very effective till now, the Librium.

I struggle against voices. Hampering, headachy . . .

Brief respite . . . during which I now remember that someone telephoned; the telephone rang for quite a long time without my answering. It is only now that I realize I confused the ringing with the confusion of noises, voices, and illusory impressions which were assailing me.

I want to write again. The impression that someone is watching me, perhaps with a touch of impudence. Probably because since I took the Librium I am not the same as I was. My "self," which was not up to dealing with the situation, is affected. Cowardly conduct which was subject to mockery. One might have hoped for more. That is why, though it doesn't mean that the childish and mocking (?) jeers I hear are intended for me, they correspond to the situation. It was absurd to take so many precautions and now this jeering starts. What might evoke ridicule leads, by the dramatizing common in such states, to the actual perception of jeering. Henceforth, without being intentional (as a paranoiac would think), these jeers nonetheless fit the situation. They fit, provoked by what has been my attitude and by my present embarrassment, that of someone . . . at whom one could jeer if one knew . . . etc.

Librium is certainly not to be advised. No effect. It has merely put me in a false situation.

Parched (by what?), I drink, taking huge gulps. Then remain sitting at the table, not knowing what to do next, the glass facing me. The offensive of things begins, begins all over again. The glass wants to drink me.

The raisins, the tube of glue watch me, or will watch me . . .

Difficulty with writing. I drop the pen and look for another one. There are several, and some ball-points, and two rather than one, and three rather than two, on my night table beside me.

My consciousness cannot grasp what I see, my eye distinguishes but my mind sees all as a whole, is slow in individualizing one after the other the elements of the field of vision, in recognizing the objects. It is an effort to have to apprehend them rapidly and successively with their attributes, their function, their signification. To identify them. I labor at this table in order to set aside the gray thing (the eraser) I do not need, the white flat object (the pad), no need, the red, faceted rod (the pencil), no need.

All these reports I must make to myself exhaust me. At last, I have what I need, within reach. Onward. I quickly write a word. It is the word, it is not the word. I see that it is not the word. I must have used the wrong letters. But where? It doesn't look right. I see that a great deal is wrong with the word, but I cannot manage to distinguish, to find in the general appearance of something wrong the specific location of mistakes. Yet I do not want to start from so defective a basis. Finally it becomes clear.

The word, similar and yet dissimilar at the same time, has again become, after groping and displacement of letters, the right word—and "ddificcult" becomes, after laborious investigations, an ordinary "difficult."

Too many things are going on around me. Evening has come. The lamps have been lit. Not too many. Enough. As usual.

I see avenging hands reaching toward me. They gesture threateningly.

Filled, filled to bursting with energy, with aggression.

Jerkily they extend, advance, point at me, indignantly aim at me.

Passionate, maddening, unbearable, pulling back and again reaching out toward me, without stopping.

This group, filled with hostility, never gives me a respite.

Fascinated at first, I then make every effort to stop seeing them, to escape these accusing hands. But I find them on my right, sometimes here, sometimes there. It is difficult to give my mind another direction, to pretend that this furious and aggressive accusation against me is not going on.

Not easy.

Having managed it (not completely, not all the time), gradually recovering, step by step, my normal "self," my self from before, certain reflections begin to occur to me. The urge to grasp and observe these enemies better, in order to learn what precisely they are doing, what they are like.

From the start I was shaken, thrown back, deeply upset at seeing them so aggressive, so furious, so indefatigably returning to the charge, invariably violent and hostile. (They must have some reason. What could it be?)

Best, observe them—permit them to return.

So be it. At that very moment, as though wrenched out of

the dark by an elastic thread, they are back where they were, and again acting outraged, pursuing me with gestures and surely also insults, though I do not hear them. Again I suffer the impact, and my powers are weakened. But the respite has allowed me to understand that I must *observe* at all costs. Hold my ground. Not yield.

And then I begin, not so much seeing them better (they are invariably a group of almost indistinguishable, unidentifiable elements) but—this had escaped me before—observing their style, a style which gives me food for thought.

These insistent hands, these violently outstretched arms, these threatening gestures can hardly be called natural; they recall, rather, the way people threaten in Italian operas, or in certain huge romantic paintings of historical subjects. They are hands meant to be seen as threatening, hands specially devised for a spectacle of admonition, not hands trying to threaten me in person. Of course they move, more or less, in my direction, but they are so theatrical, too theatrical to be concerned with just me, to be addressing someone like me effectively. To curse me in cadence with gestures so excessive, so eloquent, to cluster in a group (a well-formed, well-composed, too well-composed group) in order to pursue me with maledictions . . . is too much. Obviously, at first sight, I was appalled.

Now I notice that they are not convincing. These splendid melodramatic attitudes all for my benefit, to convince me of my villainies . . . I ought to be amazed that I fell for it. The real problem is that I fell for it. Vaguely I begin to realize this, without as yet grasping it fully. On the other hand, I see more distinctly the flaws of the group pursuing me. A group that now appears as capable only of one or rather two attitudes—indubitably of threat, and of hostile indignation. Attitudes exercised in cadence, and at a certain distance. Not letting me catch my breath. Pursuing me, sometimes more from the right, sometimes from the center, chasing . . . without chasing me.

To be persecuted: this happens only if you let yourself be judged by others, by a "superego" consisting of others. I have long since refused to give others this right. What do they know, after all, these judgers? Yet to be "pursued" is like being "persecuted." What is happening? I realize that I am not so integrally myself as usual, and that this has occurred not only because of the fact that I have pusillanimously (?) taken Librium.

Perhaps, in fact, I feel "out of line." Without having formally promised never again to take a hallucinogen, I have, to allay the fears of someone dear to me, shown that I am through with such things, and that I no longer take them, to all intents and purposes. Although there has been no promise . . . The fact remains that I may be blaming myself in relation to her though she would not blame me herself, being too tactful to do such a thing without embarrassment. I must have blamed myself in her name, in other words tormented myself, in other words pursued myself with reproaches, for reproaches always assail you severally. Several aspects, several ways, and there was . . . a pursuit. Danger of not being unassailable. So I saw hands, the hands which are pursuing me, persecuting hands. Hashish madness, like normal madness, runs immediately to excesses, to dramatic attitudes, to melodrama, being overexcited, expressionistic in its manifestations.

Feeling vaguely reprehensible, I have yielded to this theatricalization.

Never take drugs when you feel at fault.

Persecution will follow. It is the theatricalization of self-reprimand.

It is not foolish to say that it is the hallucination which produces madness and not madness which produces the hallucination; it is the dramatized and enacted, performed, hysterical, and unrelenting spectacle which drives mad the person who had only vague things to blame himself for, and perhaps did not even know what they were. The tremendous and incessant spectacle maddens the man who otherwise would be able to endure it.[4]

. . . .

Enough reflection. The spectacle had overwhelmed me. I have exorcised its power. Yet I do not escape unharmed.

Fatigue on every level.

The surroundings become crowded, charged in various ways. Overcharged. Natural things become hard to notice.

To notice is not only to perceive. It is to take a snapshot—not only a visual snapshot, but a mental one. More than that, it is to have an attitude toward reality, once it is understood.

4. On other occasions, I have seen dramatic figures of a different sort. In the days when there were official directors of conscience, bishops, priests, or pastors, those who had, or believed they had, much to reproach themselves for saw the grimaces of beings with hideous demoniac aspects. It was grandiloquent, excessive, but it carried weight, the demoniac faces never failed to appear at moments of distress, malnutrition, suffering. Even without faith, they still resuscitate archetypal or primitive images, but their power not being sustained by a great context of belief, the puppet can sometimes be discovered within them. Not often. Could one have done so in the past? The stronger the dose of the drug, the more terrifying the figure. As soon as it is *very* terrifying, you lose out. It has a hold over you. You are its "antiphon."

Too much life hereabouts.

Intersections of perplexity.

So this dose was a strong one after all; its effect is still with me, undiminished.

All right. It must be endured.

Comings and goings, in the corridor, from one room to the next. Wherever it is, anywhere, I feel I am "on the bias."

In what part of the world am I at the same time that I am here?

. . . .

Visions.[5]

5. Of which no trace remains.

B. *Further Alienating Transitions*

The silence is beginning to change.

Around me something—something extreme, tenuous, indefinable, a stirring in all directions, coming closer. In the vicinity, a multitude advances.

The solitary room has turned into a surge of murmurs, the kind which emanate from a household.

Words which assume an extreme value. At the moment, the word "thousands."

In a travel magazine lying open on the table, a girl glides down a snowy slope. But I'm the one who's there, gliding down. No, it's the girl who's in me, now I'm in her.

I cannot stabilize the situation. I am the mountain, then the slope, then only "descending." I am continually swept on into mystifying transitional stages where I cannot hold on to what is mine, where each thing's property is transitory—properties of the girl, the place, their meeting, gliding which drops me between my points of reference, nothing to hold on to, or so little, sometimes in the girl, sometimes in the snow, sometimes in the cold and the speed, they too unrelated and unable to retain their attributes and their individuality which trickles away and vanishes without any specific possessor.

Something in my head opens to Knowledge. Something new. A zone wakens for the first time.
. . . .
Confronted with the admirable, I admire less, I yield instead to its invasion.

Without moving, I sense instead.

I sink into "feeling" without interrupting myself by admiration, by approval. I continue descending into feeling.

Pleasure of opening up to understanding. Enlightened, incandescent thoughts, thoughts as it were detached from Truth.

Washed by the good vibrations. I receive the illuminating shower.
. . . .
Certainly, in the future, I shall understand better.

The room changes, changes further. A wall appears. An unknown garden, which immediately seems quite familiar, a vast garden is at my feet. I am on a balcony. How can this be? And all so natural, so unpreventable . . .

It is now some six times, within an hour or half an hour, that my room has changed,[6] totally changed.

6. To speak of visual hallucination or pseudo-hallucination is by the very use of these words beside the point. They seem to suggest that a room, or a place, a piece of furniture, is quite fixed, solid, that sight ceaselessly consolidates and that another

What happens, what appears, makes no use whatsoever of the configuration of my room; it is not a visual illusion starting from a chair which might vaguely resemble a tree trunk,[7] or from a rug which might look like a gravel path. No, right in the middle of my room, where there had been nothing, not even a slipper or a jar, rises a wall, and nothing in the walls or the furnishings heralded the arrival of a balcony, a broad terrace open to the sky, where people are talking without paying any attention to me.

The spots least likely to create an illusion, the bookcase, the radiators, open up, and wide prospects have no difficulty traversing the woodwork, taking the place of my room, which vanishes in proportion, which I cannot preserve. Other places force themselves upon me, invade, annihilate this one. I am not at all pleased by this. I cannot underesti-

---

visual element (real or imaginary) is necessary to conquer them or to take their place.

Unfortunate notion of those who believe in the primacy of the visual, who seek to begin everything with what is seen.

A way of being, an attitude—that is how I begin. It is because I no longer have the strength to be alone in my room that I am on a balcony, a terrace, and that boys and girls are talking close to me. Because I have no autonomy, I have people around me. My lack of interior consistency has summoned up these open places, these people unconcerned with me, but whose proximity is welcome to me, to my condition which "answers" to it, the condition of a man lacking the strength of solitude. To call this a visual illusion is still being on the wrong track, since it is only *secondarily visual*. The impact of an impression, excluding the others, and in two or three seconds the scene is visualized. Before seeing it, we are in it. First and foremost, we are there.

If this state is called hallucinatory, it is to conjure up the magician delirium, which however is in no way a necessary concomitant, any more than a quiescent somnambulism.

Around these "scenes" of the unreal, so varied, so tenuous, so natural, it is very difficult to establish "frames."

7. And from there would extend to the woods, the countryside...

mate the fact that it is by the defeat of what surrounds me that they are here.

. . . .

Unable to prevent this, I stand up and go out into the hallway.

Not for long. Sometimes one soon exhausts the powers one had supposed to be enormous. I shall lie down once again, at least sit down.

Fine. Let's go back. But the door resists. The door is locked from inside. What is this new mystery? I am filled with fear.

What if all the doors were locked from inside now? What if they all were locked behind me? There is something here which cannot be, but which is. Why impossible? Then I realize that I cannot quite understand why it would be impossible. I lack the power of *thinking through*. I give up before reaching the goal, exhausted, at loose ends, in a way that would surely appear absurd to others. This thought, easier than reasoning, leaves me up in the air.

Not wanting to continue in the direction of reasoning, of thinking through, since I reach nothing definitive, I take a few steps toward the other door, by walking through another room. I approach the door, though careful not to try it to find out whether it is locked.

This is my last chance. I am not going to risk losing it so soon . . . I need some respite . . .

The absurdity of what should by now be overwhelmingly obvious still does not strike me. It has too powerful an adversary, occupying my own brain.

Here, I suppose, is why:

The impression of "locked doors" is prevalent in me at this moment, dominating all the rest, which becomes insignificant. Finding myself in front of a locked door—that is my reality at this moment, not a memory but a prolonged, perpetual reality, an irreducible reality. Another door, similar and simultaneously, keeps me from re-entering myself, a self to which, whatever I do, I cannot return.

Have I become suggestible? So it would seem. There must be an overruling thought, a thought not long in existence but ruling all the same, which rules out any other thought in me that might deal with this situation.

Certainly a strong thought. Yet it would not even need to be so strong, since it is the only one, and since no other thought will compete with it in order to deal with the problem.

The periodically recurring notion of the absurdity of the situation does not affect my conviction, that is, the hegemony of this impression which imprisons me, which tells me I will find a locked door.

Yet, to get it over with, I step forward, ready for the worst, and turn the knob; the door opens, the spell is broken, and at that moment I remember that contrary to my habits and to my initial intention, I had left the room by this other door in order to go into this room where I had nothing to do and which I must have walked through without realizing it, in order to get into the hallway.

There, then, is the main reason for my derangement, this double lacuna in my memory, which could only be filled by correct reasoning, a *thinking through* that would enlighten me. I was far from that. As I returned to my room, I still had the impression of someone who dissolves magic spells as he passes through them.

Again I caution myself.

There are notions I reject, words too (which I avoid writing), for they do not favor my security. I may not think of them, for I would obey them or it would be quite exhausting to resist them.

. . . .

Inner void.

I glance vaguely at the ground, the floor at my feet, the rug.

Suddenly the rug opens. Not entirely.

It consists of a figure repeated sixteen times in different wools. Only one begins to open to life. The rest of the rug has not moved, it stays motionless, opaque. Only one figure moves, lives, becomes the site of a scene, an extremely lively, even fierce scene.

In this enclave, two warriors are fighting with a skill and a speed that take your breath away.

It is as if some (historical?) information were given me, me alone, in this enclave, about this spectacle.

While amazement rises within me, the phenomenon stops, the rug becomes a rug again. Wholly rug. It is over.[8]

I want to describe it to someone. Right away. I need to make it known, to communicate it. I have become so garrulous! I can't keep anything to myself! How unlike me that is!

I telephone. Ordinary remarks. Not a word of what I was planning to say. Something, a curious placidity at the other end of the wire,[9] warns me that I might not be understood. My own words, once I hear them, abash me. My remarks are

8. As described here, this spectacle appears somewhat brief, though it was not so. The page with the descriptive notes has disappeared, with a good many others. All this happened some two or three years ago, and the apparently "unforgettable" remains in darkness without notes.

9. Yet I am talking to a boy whom I normally regard—and with reason—as high-strung and quite the opposite of a tranquil temperament.

not alone in my mouth. Another voice than mine makes its way into my voice, a traitor. I stop. Strange. Dismaying. Discouraging. With a word, which was not mine, a voice, also alien, has tried to intervene.

I turn on the radio. A symphony. I listen to it. Now, no matter how I adjust the knobs, a stringed instrument, though part of the string section, stands out, emerges, as if instead of being on the stage with the others, it were playing right in my ears. Jarring, meaningless, not at all characteristic of the B.B.C. ensembles or of what is played in the sober concert halls of London, and besides the whole orchestra sounds uneven, crude, chaotic, which is quite unlikely, considering the source. Incredibly abrupt notes . . . and imprecise. More like village musicians who had not practiced, had no one to lead them, had been given up as incapable of improvement.

Entrances delayed, notes never played together, no, it's incredible.

So an orchestra (and one of the greatest) is imprecise, consistently imprecise, clumsy in execution. I would never have believed it.

I pick up a book. Hard to read. I skip a chapter. Suddenly the shadow of the pages I have turned, shifting, becomes large, too large, falls across me, across my life. A shadow that is unbearable, heavy, crushing, which I must be rid of as soon as possible.

. . . .

Rest. No. No. Restlessness. RESTLESSNESS, which does not relent.

Ugliness repels me, though ordinarily it interests me as something rich, revealing. It becomes repulsive, almost immediately repulsive. Yes, I must "repulse" it, cast from me the image of the ugly person. It is too insistent, violating my vital space.

I see this singular faucet open now: myself living.

Terrifying. Terrifying.

. . . .

I hear the sound of some Hindu musical instrument. Unaccompanied, sonorous. Magnificent! Profound.

And so on.

Not tremendously dramatic. The drama is in the texture, in the deflecting texture which never comes to an end.

Dozens of deflections, of micro-deflections. The illusory passes, followed by another kind of illusory.

The role of the minutest illusions is by no means secondary; in alienation, it permits the frequent appearance of the "major scene," which otherwise might be resisted.

Mental disturbance would not exist without the overabundance of insignificant deflections of attention and deflections of reality and deflections of authority.

It is the multitude of these micro-operations, invisible on the surface, evasive and destructive, which initiate the great tragedies, the great deliriums of madness. And it is by them that madness persists.

IV. THE PRESENCES WHICH SHOULD NOT BE THERE

*Madness is an endless hoax,
in which the alienated subject
is ceaselessly transcended.*

N. in his room, lying on a couch.

Around him, presences. An impression of presences; presences which should not be there.

He tries to read. It is evening. The lamplight falls on his book, his hands, the couch. Yet reading becomes difficult. Something somewhere has changed. He looks up from the text. The room has become larger—noticeably larger. It is not his room. This one—suddenly he recognizes it—is over sixty miles away, in the Grand Duchy, in a great mansion he has occasionally visited, the estate of a great lady. She might come in. She came in often. How easy it is without moving to move from one room to another, from afar. He would never have believed it. Unbelievably easy, and instantaneous. Alarming.

Without stirring, N. goes back to reading. In a sense, he knows it's the best thing to do.

And soon he is back in his room in Paris. Without looking up from the book, he's sure of it. If he could go on reading . . .

He hears the door opening, gently opening. But again he is no longer in his room. Spacious, that's the room he is in now, particularly spacious, of an unexpected shape, oblong, manorial, a gallery in a palace rather than a room; yet right away he is quite relaxed here, perfectly attuned to his surroundings, and remains stretched out without a trace of embarrassment, "at home."[1]

Despite its unusual shape it is a perfectly natural, familiar room, and he is perfectly natural within it, not moving, his book open before him, which he picks up again. All the same, shouldn't he . . . isn't there some . . . ? And the anxiety rises. He is no longer in control of something. Is no longer the master of the house. He must be under some sort of spell. But he cannot just let things go. Act—he should, he will, act.

It is not enough to read. He will write. More personal. Besides, there are things to describe.

Look, now his room is back again!

. . . .

Once he finds the paper, he begins to write.

Yet once written, these words—what can be the matter with them?—like wood that turns into ashes without the mediation of fire, without his having done anything in particular, the words have ceased to belong to the order of language.

As his writing advances across the page, the words, left behind, the loops and lines already drawn, have turned into little mounds, little tufts . . . far away. He can no longer

[1]. It is a natural room, so natural that it gives him no shock of any kind. This perfect equanimity in what is nonetheless an unfamiliar place produces an illusion, makes him think he knows it, since he has experienced not the least shock or surprise. (Now surprise is the sign always regarded as infallible of the presence of what is unknown and seen for the first time, an alien thing.)

come back to them. He can no longer read any words except the ones he has just written, and those only for an instant. Whatever he does, everything, from the top of the page, turns immediately back into space, vast, abandoned, vibrant, as if it were sandy wastes.

Yet he continues writing, but ineluctably, at the top of the page, the waste returns, invading, denaturing, covering the sheet where the words, shivering, fade away on their remote veldt.

How protect himself? He can no longer write without summoning into being a great natural sight, without this phenomenon spreading, taking over the page.

It is not always a desert, but it is always a vast expanse.

Often it is a river, a great river with rushing waters, sometimes the sea, a stormy sea bearing down upon him. Yet he goes on writing. In the presence of so much water and waves, he perseveres, and the words, though trembling, are there, written on the water yet not wet, and the river does not efface them, though they cannot efface the river either.

And as he writes, the meaning, first gradually, then rapidly, the meaning, like a sound that has been emitted, short-lived, rapidly diminishing, doomed to disappear, the meaning dies away.

. . . .

He must have dozed off, or nearly, for suddenly he is awakened, interrupted rather in his somnolence by an extremely powerful sensation, an echoing sensation. He starts to describe it. But it is impossible to recapture. Vanished! It and his recollection. No help for it. Not a trace remains. The station is past.

He picks up a book lying nearby and reads two lines. But strangely enough, it is not he who is reading but the author herself, a certain Kamala Markandaya, somewhere in Madras, whom he does not know (except that he must have seen her tiny portrait just now, on the jacket, surrounded by a brief notice), it is this woman who is reading the words to him now, at the foot of his couch, with a proud, confident expression, as though teaching him a lesson.

Odious! Absurd! And he flings the book to the floor.

Better try writing again . . . and once more he begins. He has so many things to "account for."

While he scribbles his reflections, something happens, something new.

A gap appears between what he is writing and what is in his mind . . . a gap in time, a gap which leaves room for so many things.

He sees with surprise and detachment, like a boy watching a turtle making its slow progress, he sees the long, slow chain of the words of the sentence form, extend (although he surely is writing as fast as at any other moment), he sees the writing lag almost comically behind, he sees the absurd little string of the sentence which never stops growing, taking shape laboriously, extending, seemingly endless, before it finally reaches the end, while he, as though "at leisure," inactive, having all the time in the world, elaborates ideas on his idea, the idea in the creeping sentence.

Then he suddenly has the powerful, imperative impression of someone bending over his shoulder, watching his text over his shoulder, as a spectator, an interested enthusiast who has a word of his own to offer, who pays very close attention, who follows the text, surpervises, criticizes it, reads it even before the writing is completed!

Irritating, extremely irritating . . .

Of course, if he turned his head it would be easy to see that there is no one there in fact, in flesh and blood. And what of it? What he cannot prevent is a marginal and continual intervention, active and critical, an insistent presence which does not let a single word pass without interfering, which magisterially parts the words, like a pair of doors, to insert itself among them, to introduce its own reflections, the reflections of a witness concerned with everything and generally unco-operative—and there is nothing he can do to prevent it. This presence also keeps moving, has its own powerful, unsuspected movements, advances, retreats, returns like someone really there, close enough to touch him.

The writing continues in this fashion, "supervised" by the other. Not only by one. It is now a sort of murmur, a multiple murmur, as though from a group of several who might intercede, who intercede among the words, between one word and another, between one idea and its opposite, and interrupt, and interfere, and grumble and object, and mock, and disapprove, and jeer, and say "perhaps" and "perhaps not" and "not at all," and reconsider, and do not tolerate, and argue, and dissent, and laugh, and laugh, and laugh, and hop around, and clatter about, keep clattering, meanly, increasingly, continually, incredibly.

And so his sentence, like his handwriting, under their keen and mocking attention, seems uniform, punctilious, barren, narrow, paltry, inadequate, unbearably and indefensibly laborious.

Enough!

He can go on no longer. He stops, resolute. "No more writing!"

Moreover, he closes his eyes.

And then in the darkness behind his closed eyelids, he sees violent men suddenly appear, making emphatic gestures of denial, then a horde, then a procession of dissatisfied people carrying signs, a protesting and threatening parade.

"No more" has turned into picketers!

. . . .

Will he not have a moment's peace?

Dissatisfied, seeing himself still deceived, conned, he recoils and withdraws into himself.

Peace has not returned.

His being—this is what he feels—his being is rumpled.

He hears what sounds like smothered wild laughter.

Impression of tracks everywhere, tracks and "remains."

Gasps cross, cover space. Tracks. Reality nibbled away.

Like the sound of steam blasts escaping from the engine of a locomotive some distance away, a short distance . . .

Space would have to be cleaned.

For no reason, inexplicably moved forward, as though projected, he feels a sudden, imperative craving to throw himself out of that window, the fourth-floor window.

Stupid. Absurd. But strangely, totally mobilized, he is impelled forward. The act, the acts, unbelievingly experienced, unbelievably compelling, appear and unite within him, as powerful as if he performed them, as if in reality he threw off the blanket and got up, and jumped out of bed, and hurriedly took the six or seven steps that separate him from the window, and drew back the curtains, and opened the window wide, ready to leap onto the sill, and then did leap up onto it, and standing there leaned out over the void, leaning farther, farther, too far, and fell . . .

. . . .

He tries to divert himself. It is urgent, essential, that he be diverted immediately. He turns on the floor lamp, the night lamp, then draws the curtains, both pairs, shifts the armchairs, moves everything he can, in order to obstruct the dangerous path to the outside, to block it with a chair, a table, anything.

The path must be cut off, the dangerous, ever open, tempting path which continues to symbolize the path of suicide. Strange, this word, which he does not recognize, although no other is appropriate. He has no desire for suicide. It plays no part in his thoughts.

Yet, it is exhausting to struggle against the compelling image, compelling, constantly returning, against the lure of the window, against the unknown which impels him toward the window, toward the void, though he still has no desire to kill himself, as he still may if this continues.

He suffers as he would if someone had actually pushed him toward the window just now, a movement from which he might have barely escaped at the last possible moment.

Although he has not moved, he feels as though he had narrowly escaped death.

The reading . . . this Kamala Markandaya, very useful this time, who has not changed, who as a good Hindu believes in and tenaciously pursues her cause. Her continuity will save him . . .

Save?

No, he is not saved, and suddenly he drops everything, quickly dresses, and virtually tears the door from its hinges in order to leave the room of his temptation faster.

When he had to go downstairs, things went more slowly, he had to be more careful, it was more difficult to make certain gestures, certain movements, to proceed down the spiral stairwell where a new dizziness overtakes him.

At last he is downstairs. And now outside.

In his heart of hearts he knows immediately: the street will be too much for him (too multifarious, too fluid), but he is there. He will stay where he is, at least for a few minutes. He is not going to give up right away.

Passers-by, no easy matter. And these presences moving on all sides. Presences, multiplication of presences.

In the street (but to begin with, it is the wrong street), in the street (a street that looks as though it is waiting, lying in wait for the passers-by, trying to keep an eye on them), in the street, then (a street lying in wait, doubtless to play some nasty trick), he is not comfortable. He isn't walking properly. Not really. Not quite. Yet that isn't the main thing. The main thing is this street, which has "leftover" space, space he doesn't know what to do with, far too much space.

Especially because he will soon have to cross it. He stops, considers at length whether he really is going to cross it. It is so complicated to cover the surface of a street like this. And in the middle, the void . . .

Yet it is a street he has crossed, so to speak, every day.

Not only is the street strangely diminished, squeezed to a disproportionately long and narrow size, but the house fronts are also no longer quite the same. House fronts so elaborately detailed, so richly ornamented, so gaudy, indicative of . . . but . . . of what?

Besides, he does not really recognize it. Of course if it is not this street, which one could it possibly be? This is the only street in the neighborhood that ought to be here. But how peculiar it looks where it is now, quite out of place. It occupies space with a sort of absence, and yet too ostentatiously to be that either. Still, a street that substituted for it, or was running close by and parallel to it, a street which to this moment he had not noticed—a preposterous thought. Someday he would have seen it. Inevitably. Inevitably? Is he sure?

Also he has to walk farther than usual in order to cross where he wanted to (they must have enlarged it then, widened it? When?) An ordeal. Must it be endured? But how escape it? By what means? Like a trick someone had played on him, crude, proliferating, enormous. This is mad. And by what means?

He leaves the street, takes another, a smaller, calmer, narrow one, too narrow, cramped, with sloping houses. Too much. Much too much. Strangely set, too. The top floor, the fourth and fifth floors, a strong push would surely send them toppling. It is intolerable to have to pass under them, with the risk of a floor and a roof that might come crashing down on you. Of course you don't hear of them falling often. But who hears about everything? It's alarming. It's disturbing. It will surely happen someday—they'll fall. Someday soon. And what if it were today? How pass by without anxiety? Don't people even lift their heads? But, as a matter of fact, there's hardly anyone in this street now. People avoid it . . .

N. turns away at once, turns again. This time he enters a large thoroughfare with heavy traffic. Tired. He gets in line at a bus stop.

Noises! Noises in every direction. Noises which penetrate deep into his head. Ah, there's a bus! Ticket, money, pocket, change, give, receive, get on, enter, check, count, announce, exchange, calculate, answer, return change, tickets, papers, actions, actions that have to follow a certain sequence, otherwise they can't be performed successfully . . . actions, which at this moment are no longer performed unconsciously, which several times he nearly fails to work out, which raise problems, which arouse expectations, which are disturbing, which create complications—which produce a pull, which hypnotize—which call for your attention, which detract. Commuters. Businessmen. Women. Wrinkles. The wrinkles of advanced age. Very deep wrinkles. Oh, when women laugh . . . How dare they? Sheaves of wrinkles, stars of wrinkles. Why so many wrinkles today? Puckers. Like the cracked bark of old oaks . . .

Are they watching him? Glances, at first fleeting and casual, now revert to him more often, scrutinize him, once repeatedly, not staying fixed on him, scattering, then returning . . .

By accident? Deliberately? Does he look strange, different?

He also has the impression that people can read his mind. Sooner or later someone might take advantage of him, if he keeps on exposing himself . . .

. . . .

Back home. Exhausted.

But the street within him is not yet entirely exhausted.

Past noises keep passing by.

Murmurs continue to murmur.

As though the voices heard earlier, instead of fading, as they do, as they must do, had remained suspended, and like curtains sliding on rods, from time to time parted again, moved forward, swerved, once again drew near.

There is no silencing of the noises.

Voices, heard in the street half an hour ago, recur in his room, revive, grow, then fade, then grow louder again, closer, increasing in volume, diminishing again, in an almost soothing rhythm. Dizziness. Waves. Waves.

There is no abatement. Again he resorts to reading. This time, it is an elementary text, a boys' magazine, abundantly illustrated, "instructive." He begins. It seems to be going all right.

Immersed in reading that "Archimedes lost his life during the siege of Syracuse at the time of the final assault, when he was struck by a Roman soldier," suddenly noises reach his ears, close-by, loud, resounding noises—the noises of the battle. Terrifying screams. Swords clashing. He hears violent blows striking the shields, walls collapsing, stones falling. As though he were out there in the open, in that city, in 212 B.C. It is the groans of the wounded, in particular, that have taken him to the spot. The uproar leaves him dizzy. Though he has stopped reading, the "pitched" battle continues savagely.

. . . .

A battle story obviously not being what is needed at this point, because of the noise which curiously emerges from it and absorbs all his attention and space itself, after a moment's rest he turns to another text, a religious one this time—more appropriate to his purpose, and surely more appeasing: the description of the arrival of a foreign lama in a Nepalese monastery. Suddenly, once again, reading is rudely interrupted. The loud, brazen, magnificent sounds from great Tibetan trumpets resound powerfully, transforming his room into a high Himalayan valley, filled with the smell of rancid butter and an atmosphere of magic.

Reading having proved quite impossible, he gives up and keeps his eyes closed. Once he thinks he has rounded the Cape of noises, he opens his eyes again and notices a postcard, received the night before, from J., in Honfleur, as the photo (the lighthouse) indicates; on the reverse side he reads, distractedly, "best wishes" and that the weather is humid and cloudy.

At these words, he is there. Out to sea, near the harbor. He hears the foghorn, several long blasts, and the sea mist makes him shiver . . .

. . . .

Leaving this noise behind, N. comes to a most important warning about . . . let's see, about . . . But as he returns to it, only a second later, it is forgotten. Impossible to remember it. All he recovers is the word WARNING. Everything stops there, with the sight of the printed word. WARNING. No use insisting, only the word returns, the wall of the word.

. . . .

And what about eating something?

The table nearby is set. He set it a little while ago, rather casually. He sits down, begins to eat, but the bread basket is far from his plate, and the butter as well, and the salt too, at the far end of the table, almost hidden.

Nor is his glass in front of him, nor the knife where it should be, nor the pitcher of water. A setting out of order which, from fatigue, he did not correct, so that now, not finding the usual objects in their place, he gets lost when he needs something. His hand starts out and each time moves in the wrong direction; belatedly, at half course, he shifts, corrects as best he can, remembering only vaguely, each erroneous result causing him great effort, within a growing impression of mental confusion, of failing attention, of dizziness, of misery, of powerlessness.

The hand wanders, gives up.

During one of these tedious "broken trajectories" he inadvertently drops a glass of water, which breaks. Although no one is there, a wild, mocking, sarcastic laugh responds immediately to this clumsiness.

Disconcerted, disgusted, he leaves the dining room to lie down on the couch. Perhaps everything may still work out . . .

. . . .

Awakening.

An unpleasant taste in his mouth. very strong, horrible: ink. Will he ever be able to get rid of it? He sees nothing which resembles ink. But isn't that the taste you have when you've been poisoned with arsenic? What does that mean? And this smell of something rotten? Putrefaction? Already? He gets up to go brush his teeth. Forgetting that he is naked, he goes into the bathroom, where, catching himself in the mirror, meeting in the eyes "facing him" the unprepared eyes of another, of a witness who might happen to be there, and who, unlike himself, could not find the situation natural, he draws back in shame, as though caught out, as if before a reprimand or the scandalized gesture of someone deeply shocked by his impropriety.

He moves too much. It was the same a little while ago at the table: serving himself, eating, shifting objects, his gestures, because of his clumsiness and his blunders, provoke criticism (which, instead of being interior, seems external). He has just understood. He must remain calm. He had already suspected as much awhile back. That he must keep entirely still. Otherwise he will see (or feel) the criticism, the gestures of criticism directed against him.

Keeping still, in order to prevent interference, in order not to call "another" into being.

. . . .

And what about a trip, taking a plane, starting his life over again? What if he called to reserve a seat on the plane, now, immediately. Yes or no? Yes?

As he hesitates—he has never been the least bit attracted by America—as he tries to keep from sliding down the slope (but already the momentum is in command, he is thinking about luggage, passport, checkbook, telephone . . .) a fly appears.

A big fly, a fly making huge circles under the ceiling, between the ceiling and him. A fly of extreme significance which seems to have come for him, to warn him. Meaningful, a fly of fate. A fly to give him the answer, give him the signal whether or not to leave. In the meantime the fly, without hurrying, without alighting, keeps circling. It is not going to give the answer immediately, before it is ripened . . . when it is ready the fly will land either on the window, signifying that he should leave, or on the table or the blanket if he should stay . . .

While he waits, here, in his dressing gown, for the fly verdict, someone rings, rings again, someone is coming to visit him. It is V., who has come with T. Odd: why should he come to see him looking so strange?

Why not just have come? Why that cavernous voice? When there's no depth to him anyway . . . He doesn't realize it. But what if he were doing it intentionally? What if he were teasing N.? There's no doubt that he's trying to talk in a different way, with a new voice. Quite ridiculous. Who could have advised him to do such a thing . . . advice he's following so gullibly? Perhaps someone told him he seemed too frivolous, too superficial. Or perhaps he's trying to suggest to N. that he's not really profound, plays at being deep when he's only narrow-minded?

That can't be it either. The cavernous tone of voice is too monotonous.

But what has he come for, sick as he obviously is, though he doesn't mention that? Who goes visiting when he looks like that—gray, an ashen gray? And his corpselike jaw is about to drop. It's not holding up any longer. He should be home and in bed, instead of being out in such a condition.

And T.—what an idea to come with a sick man! She isn't comfortable. She's trying to act a part. Or are they accomplices? Those looks they keep exchanging . . .

And her voice has changed too—how does she manage to sound like that? What a pair! Phonies.

They've left. At last!

He will go out too. The room is polluted.

He leaves. Lingers a bit next to a tree on the avenue.

. . . .

Absence. Long absence. He "comes to himself" sitting on a bench. The harmony which now fills him is indescribable. He experiences a rightness, a rightness of extraordinary scope, a rightness of which he had no idea.

Everything is fine, fine as it should be, magnificently fine. It is unthinkable that anything in the world could be better. Everything is related in an almost suffocating benevolence, utterly benevolent, perfect, right. He is overcome. Flooded. His channels are filling. A supreme kind of mercy. And an illumination. Immensity proceeding from an unbelievable Immensity: a cosmic insemination occurs. An immense calm has set in. A fusion of contradictions. There are no more obstacles. Like an infinitely calm body of water, which periodically stirs, moving imperceptibly . . . How disarming, the Infinite. And this Immensity seeks its course.

And the ABSOLUTE calls, summons, solicits him, enters him. Gives him strength. Directs him, fills him, "swells him." Too much! Too much! To bursting. He has a mission to fulfill, a mission in relation to the WORLD. An urgent mission. The message he must deliver (of which he must also deliver himself) is an emergency message: everyone without exception must hear it. It is as though it were tearing him apart. He cannot bear to keep it to himself any longer. Yet he must. An imperative message. A message for which he finds no words, for which there is no word, no word in any language.

Only in the MIND. ONLY when he is totally transformed into mind will he be able to deliver the message.

All the time the message swells, swells, suffocates him; the everlasting, exorbitant, infinite, infinitely shattering message.

. . . .

V. DIVESTMENT THROUGH SPACE

For some time I had intended taking c.i.[1] at a high altitude, to contemplate a mountain sky line. I had come for that reason to this place, to see if there would be any effect, and what it would be. Several days go by. Finally I take the once-coveted substance. Time passes. Nothing. I feel no change. The mountains before me keep the same appearance. My health is perhaps overrestored. Then, meals sometimes having a catalytic effect, I go down to the dining room.

The dark came too soon. I must have miscalculated.

I had hoped, upon returning, to find the mountains again, even more impressive in the twilight. When I returned, they were no longer there. Even the loftiest summits had ceased to be visible. Every last one had disappeared in the night. Dismayed, my journey a failure, alone on the vast balcony in front of my room, with nothing before me to contemplate, no longer knowing what to do, I lingered stupefied.

1. One of the psychedelic substances, among the oldest known.

Finally, before going back inside I raise my head. A black sky filled with stars stretched out all around me. I plunged into it. It was extraordinary. Instantaneously stripped of everything as though of an overcoat, I passed into space. I was projected into it, I was hurled into it, I flowed into it. I was violently seized by it, irresistibly.

. . . .

An utterly unsuspected marvel . . . Why hadn't I known of it earlier? After the first minute of surprise, it seemed altogether natural to be borne off into space. And yet, how many times had I looked at skies as beautiful and more beautiful without any effect other than a sincere and futile admiration? Admiration: antechamber, nothing but an antechamber. Once again I verified the effect.

What I was experiencing was very different from admiration, an entirely different scale of response.

What exactly? It is not easy to grasp. As though torn from the earth, feeling myself carried irresistibly upward, borne ever farther by a marvelous invisible levitation, into an endless space, which *could* not end, which was incommensurable with myself, which kept drawing me into it, I soared up, higher and higher, inexplicably inspired, though without, of course, ever being able to reach any destination. Besides, what destination?

It could have been awful. It was an effulgence.

The static, the finite, the solid had seen their day. There was nothing left of them, or almost nothing. Divested, I rose, propelled; stripped of possessions and attributes, stripped even of all recourse to the earth, all sense of place being lost—an unimaginable divestment, which seemed almost absolute, since I was unable to find anything it would not have taken from me.

Surely, I had not seen, not really seen the sky, before. I

had resisted it, viewing it from the other side, from the side of the earth, from what is solid, if opposite.

This time, the shore having collapsed, I was sinking in. Dizzily, I sank upward.

The sky—I was in it. At last we were in contact.
And I continued to observe it, if the word "observe" applies to an abyss into which one is flung and from which nothing any longer separates you.

The surface of a star-studded sky, by its sudden disappearance, had revealed its endless depth. It did not cease deepening.
From time to time I averted my eyes, trying to compose myself "against it," since I was reaching the limit of what I could bear as a loss of self. Having then recovered myself in a certain fashion, I looked at it again and immediately it overpowered me once more, "overrunning me" at full speed. An ineffable invasion. A tidal wave which suddenly overwhelms the earth, but it was the sky, the enormous sky which sovereignly entered.
I received the sky and the sky received me.
At the same time, I was in an extraordinary expansion. Space turned me into space . . .
In a great many other ways, it came to me. Space was everywhere.

Sometimes, in order not to yield to it on too many levels, I tried, by cutting off other communicating lines, to limit myself to the precise view of the small, stellar dots shining in the firmament, a view which, since the excess was within me, I then received no longer parsimoniously, as usual, but superabundantly, beyond measure. To such a degree that, my head thrown back in order to confront more sky, I *felt* the vision, so deeply and powerfully did it penetrate me—"up to the ears, up to the occiput." These are the words which imposed themselves on me during those moments when, stirring and resisting, I tried to be no longer a dot swept on by space, but a witness who, wrecked, still uses his eyes.

That was the effect this view produced on me then, but soon, my strength, which I intended to concentrate for this purpose, reached the limit of its resistance and was giving way; I detached myself from the "restricted" spectacle, my head again lost in the gaping maw of space which swallowed me up, higher and higher.

In a sort of nausea that turned into delight, I drifted, swaying beneath the remote and shifting stars that momentarily resembled the lights of distant ships glimpsed at night pitching up and down on the surging sea, lights which here would have been those of galactic vessels navigating the ocean of the boundless. This ocean spread in all directions, nothing else mattered.

Space was permanent. It was not unvarying. In fact, it varied constantly. For a long time, it was on the increase. Spaces beyond this space formed themselves anew, spaces which after some time engendered others, and still others, so that each new kind of space canceled the preceding one, even depriving it of something or other, making it more immaterially space, purified space, with nothing heterogeneous left.

Space, space beyond everything. Contemplation. Face to face and not only face to face. Everywhere I coincided with it, meeting it on all sides. Untranscendable and with no salient feature, nothing the mind could take hold of. Yet there was constant exchange. To contemplate, I realized, was not what I had thought. Contemplation is being received.

And still I endured this distance, this deluge of infinity.
As one endures the evening's cold.
The distance had passed into another class, and I too had passed into another class, the pupil I had been was no longer the same. Moreover, "expansive" rather than concentrated, in cold illuminations.
Space shared me with nothing else.
A matchless time elapsed.

The sky was no longer a dome. The earth was no longer a foundation. They were no longer to be united. No temple now—there was no longer any necessity for a temple.
The traveler was awed. The participant was shaken. Yet the incorruptible observer was there. Such were the three faces of the person who nevertheless no longer felt like a person.
Space, space. Space was my only reality. Were it not for some surreptitious glances downward I might have believed I had been transformed into space.
The space that had been released, freed, by a sovereign mechanism—would it ever let my being revert to matter? That seemed impossible. The unexpected, unbelievable affinity for the imponderable revealed, perceived, experienced in such an incredibly convincing way, would have to exist forever.

How much space I received during those hours! And not to be able to say anything about it! My basic physical unworthiness had abandoned me. leaving me acceptable to space. By allowing me this divestment, space had yielded itself up to me. Divestment: through this mysteriously opened breach space rushed into me. And I into it. Mysterious interpenetration. Opposing actions which corresponded to one another, not excluding each other.

Which exalted one another.

A growing divestment opened me to more space, which in turn, by stripping me further, prepared me for a new invasion of space. In this way I was enabled to experience more and more space as the weight dissolved within me, leaving me at once utterly impoverished and fulfilled.

The space echoed to nothing, yet answered to the essential, to everything.

I no longer had to renounce. I had not had to renounce.

The renunciation was over and done before I could have anticipated it. Within the instant, I had been stripped, without having been consulted, without having had time to face it, to be given a choice, necessarily treated as a blind person whose opinion is not asked, who in matters of transcendence is and always will be ignorant, muddle-headed, vociferous, inevitably misinformed, invariably inadequate to the occasion. But to this operation, which I had been unable to understand, which ended before I could examine it, I gave my impassioned approval, grateful, ever more rapturous, in unparalleled enthusiasm, in a fervor which only the miraculous dissipation of "weight" can give.

Relieved of all surroundings, cleansed of all consistency, of all property, of all sense of ownership, incapable of conceiving any possession around me and lacking the preliminary minimum necessary to any attachment, I was in an ecstasy of space.

He who does not know what to believe in had just received—I see no other word for it—something like a sacrament, the spatial sacrament.

As though the Infinite, to make itself manifest, had taken space for a simple and sufficient indicator, space as symbol and anthem. The corpse I had been, suddenly wakened, found itself opened as wide as an aphid which had just grown a whale's jaws, an aperture so wide it could accommodate only the immeasurable and never close again.

How wrong I had been in the past to seek transcendence in closed, narrow places, confronting objects, people, images of the limited world, over which, it is true, "it" triumphed for the moment, and quite marvelously, releasing them comically at times from the fetters of their limits. Yet objects, even with their massiveness thus transfigured, transcended, still remained present, tended to return and, actually after a short, too short time, reconstituted themselves in their density.

The sky is different. Different and superior. (For there is a hierarchy of values applicable to such spectacles.) The sky, then, by its very nature proceeds in the direction of expansion, of transcendence, of the limitless. Lacking anything reductive, anything weighty, once the barrier is crossed in a single leap, there is no longer any obstacle or any tendency to fall back later, to lapse, to distraction.

Without change, without incident, without analogy (which might create recollection, hence change) one remains plunged within.[2] To the rapture experienced it answers with a total acceptance that makes it needless to look for anything else—an immediate infinity which, to achieve transcendence, does not first have to rid itself of the finite.

Space is received as a purification.

2. The open skies remained so for me about two hours, much longer, therefore, than any of my previous "absences."

Should one become detached from it, deliberately or not, each time, returning to it, one experiences a "rush of spirituality."

How justified, I now saw, is the quest for vast horizons and towering sites, the pilgrimage to the Himalayas, or other mountains, considered as a precious, unique remedy by contemplatives seemingly above contingencies. They know the power of the incomparable springboard.[3]

In space, in distance, there is something special for the meditator.

Its impression excludes the impression of physical sensations, earthly impressions, that is, the more material, the incarnating impressions.

Contrary also to beings, to objects, to things, distance, however expanded, never becomes monstrous but simply becomes more purely itself. Its expansion occurs without detriment to one who meditates upon, who experiences it, whereas even light or heat, and sound as well, become painfully excessive, while not being equally "proper to the infinite." Consequently[4] it is (with the impression of extension itself) a privileged mode of liberation.

Extraordinary as this open sky may have been, by morning it no longer existed. It had vanished even before the end of the night. Although in actuality it could not have changed a great deal, it no longer existed. No longer do I penetrate its

3. Surely, anyone who contemplates the starry sky (or a boundless view) has an inkling of this impression and takes it in, but it becomes diluted among others, fading into a lower key. Only when it is raised to a tenfold, twentyfold magnitude does it bestow its gift of uniqueness.
4. Provided one does not try to gauge it in figures, in specific measurements (meters, light-years, etc.).

depth, into which I had penetrated so deeply. It has congealed.

The stars have returned to their places, to the configurations they appear to compose. I coldly view the apparent dimensions, their apparent radiance (that is, their relative radiance).

I am here and they are there: I have landed.

The dualizing consciousness has returned—the pluralizing, the plurilocalizing consciousness. The balcony is here, my body above it. The sky farther off. The mountain which will appear with the dawn, there! In that direction, Lausanne—over there, to the left.

The balcony is made of brick, the mountains of earth, myself of cartilage, nerve tissue, and bone, and aware of my location. Space is no more than a concept, an estimate, a given. Crammed with sensations, with expertly co-ordinated impressions and judgments, my being has only a little room left to devote to the impression of space.

In the marvelous hours I had experienced, free of all substantiation or matter, I was invested with space, invested to an unimaginable degree, to a point where we were almost identical, undifferentiated.

At such a point, the mind, receiving "self" and "nonself" equally, is within a veritable monism, and will experience its "revelation." But it may also experience the revelation of Maya, the Universal Illusion, whose manifestation here is obvious. And it may also experience the revelation of the Absolute, of the limitless Spirit. If it is of a loving nature, the mind can even experience the revelation of a love which is the unique universal reality. It may also experience the revelation of the rashly named "cosmic consciousness."

From such an immersion one often returns with dogmas. The barriers of the physical so utterly overcome, the metaphysical alone remaining and realizable, it is for metaphysical nourishment that one hungers, instantly and unbelievably, it is a metaphysical response that one impatiently craves, it is a metaphysical world that one urgently needs in order to receive the revelation included within it.

It is not absurd to think that in India, especially, the metaphysical experience (through direct action on the body) preceded the great metaphysical systems which were first elaborated in its mold, shaped to contain it.

The search for the liberation from duality, "to be no longer implicated by anything," the masterly detachment from self and from one's own actions and behavior, appear to have emerged from exceptional experiences, which served as a model.

As I see it, the revelation of divestment, the beatitude within divestment, the matchless expansion, that ineffable, incomparable nonduality, should be protected from accommodation by any system, no matter how tempting, protected from being distorted, prematurely, in controlled applications. How can one deal with fire as if those dealings would also satisfy earth?

Without preconception, without prejudices, I insisted—rightly? wrongly?—upon observing the direction which I and a certain new non-conformity of myself with myself would take, a non-conformity just beginning to manifest itself, hoping also that what had been so spectacularly destroyed and razed would not turn out right away to be back with a vengeance.

But once the ordinary was restored, reality re-established itself, insistent in its plurality which constitutes, which begins reconstituting the contradictions, the absurdities, the thousand complications and inescapable inadequacies of behavior, the stumbling blocks of the future. Legion are the bonds, and legion they reassert themselves. The habitations of bondage are invisible, and strong are the fine meshings which constitute a man's life. FAR, far now is the One, untroubled, far the sovereign state of simplicity.

VI. RAVAGED SELF-CONSCIOUSNESS

Those who have taken a powder with quasi-magical effects[1] and consider themselves quite unfettered, entirely liberated, out of this world perhaps, are still running on tracks. They submit.

Sights of unrivaled wonder, or so they suppose them to be, strangely enough belong to the same family; made up of similar elements, they are capable only of modulations.

People who consider themselves supremely liberated are in fact prisoners.

There exists a banality of the visionary world.

The spectacle of incessantly changing, astonishing figures which the particular properties of each drug affords is inescapably imposed on such people.

Fantastic as it might seem (once past the stage of geometric forms, clashing and kaleidoscopic colors), the visionary procession, itself no more than tributary, accompanies, augments, and translates the sensatory procession.

1. Visionary, hallucinogenic, and depersonalizing.

What is most marvelous in this dizzying passage of images: though apparently they are unrelated to each other and to the personality that experiences them, they effect, by means that short-circuit consciousness, and in a way that is rapidly, incessantly, immediately visualized,[2] the disappearance and excision, particle by particle, of the sensate, the loss of spatial consciousness of the body. Virtually without comprehension, the subject is party to it, dumfounded, enthralled, amazed, or agonized.

Of course there are various other occasions that cause changes and discontinuities in physical sensibilities,[3] always a disconcerting phenomenon even if it concerns only the simple breakdown of a function, fragile at best like everything pertaining to the human being who exists by virtue of his integration, the complete (though vague) consciousness he has of his body, a consciousness which may not be breached for one second without the penalty of extreme alienation.

But here, instead of simply effacing this consciousness in certain physical areas, in its entirety, in a more or less stable fashion, certain drugs (of the hallucinogenic series), by inducing polymorphous overexcitation, change this consciousness into an abstraction so tumultuous, discontinuous, and erratic that the subject feels as though he were a play-

2. . . . which as much as or more than the expression of memories, propensities, or ideas consists of straightforward or symbolic signs or even precursory signals not yet "signifying" anything, except to the expert, who is alerted by them to the absences of the sensate, before they become evident.

3. Such as accidents, epileptic auras, delirium caused by dehydration, hunger, physical pain or agony, tumors and lesions of the brain, disturbances of the inner ear, depressive psychoses, Pick's disease, etc.

thing; simultaneously—a more specific phenomenon which never fails to impress—the drugs brilliantly "dramatize" and illustrate these areas, projecting on the imagination's blackboard the dazzling film of images in motion which correspond to them—images abruptly intensified, heightened in color and power, and all this in a siteless space, in an agonizing restlessness, confronting a plurality of unfamiliar perspectives, while certain peculiarly accentuated thoughts proceed at high speed, doubling, countering, and intersecting each other like chessmen.

Yet the subject who keeps his eyes open, confining himself to immediate illusions of loss of the body's parts, will find himself confronting a more restricted phenomenon.

The intermittences of sensation, their apparent misreckonings, are not boundless.

Questioned during or immediately after these "unexampled" states, dozens and dozens of subjects say the same thing. Certain phrases, in the statement of the most diverse individuals, are interchangeable at every point.[4]

Just as there exists a certain banality of the visionary

4. See the report by Dr. A. Saavedra, in *Revista de Neuropsydiatrica*, Lima, Vol. XVI, no. 1, March 1953: "Algunas alteraciones psicopatologicas del despertar del Coma insulinique."

Also: "Alteraciones mentales producidas por la Opuntia cylindrica," by Gutierrez-Noruiega and G. Cruz Sanchez, Lima. *Revista de Neuropsydiatrica*, Vol. X, no. 24, 1947. (Experiments on thirty-two subjects.)

(According to recent studies, this Opuntia is a Trichocereus whose hallucinogenic agent is mescaline, but the remarks on the subjects remain valid.)

Also: "El esquema corporal o la psicosis lisergica," by Juan Carlos Rey. Montevideo, *Clinica Psiquiatrica*, I–II, 1959.

And especially: "Méconnaissances et hallucinations corporelles," by H. Hécaen et J. de Ajuriaguerra, Paris, 1952.

world, into which the genius and the simpleton are equally drawn, we find, in the sensationary world a certain banality in the extraordinary. What appears as infinite transformations of the body often proves to be limited to a few types.

For this sense of loss of some part of the body, whether an arm, a leg, a cheek, the neck, or the head, is almost never that of a pure and simple disappearance. Disappearing is still appearing. It is disappearing from a certain set of reference points, from centers of recognition, and from everything that is and was necessary to unite us with the limb or region of the body in a way that brings them close, that makes them our own and constant possession. Disappearing from this set of orientations, paradoxically, amounts to appearing.

Because of a deficiency, an "extra," an "other."

Any part of the body may then seem "changed," and in a changed position.

To the subject who has been put in this extraordinary state,[5] his arm, for example, may now appear in various different ways, but not in the only way he was used to and which he longs to see return.

It may, for instance, appear to him strangely remote. Or else elongated, unending, or curiously extending into furniture and objects, merging with the arm-rest of the chair. Or (but how is this possible?) as though reaching to the extremity of the world, or simply not his arm any longer, or as someone else's arm. (Moreover, with his eyes closed, he might take the arm of a person nearby for his own.) Or transsubstantiated into something unrecognizable or lost, or unconnected. An arm which no longer gives him information. Sometimes deadened, sometimes without firmness. At other times excessively, inexplicably light, ready to fly away, or just the opposite, extremely (and no less inexplic-

5. Of disturbed somatognosis.

ably) heavy; or partially invisible, reduced to one half or one third of its size, shortened, twisted, or oddly segmented, in no way corresponding to a zone of innervation and nervous sensitivity, or even doubled or tripled. An unsettling or demoralizing or maddening betrayal, owing to which he will never again reach his arm, though it is there and should not be so different from what it was before; but however often he comes back to it, holds it in his other hand, strikes it,[6] he is unable to reconstitute it properly, incapable of sensing it as entirely his own. It remains a strange, confusing "nonappendage," which keeps extending, profoundly disturbs something that is basic, rocking a foundation which should remain stable, persists as an unsettling, obsessive disturbance, an obvious malfunction which cannot be endured without a sense of instability and even a vague feeling of "misconduct." But it goes beyond that. It is an arm whose very absence eludes the mind, eludes an "expert" delimitation, is not really apprehensible, being the consequence of a cerebral operation, an archaic and animal infra-thought, suddenly revealed by its disappearance. And the fundamental deviation goes on, needles him, compels him to take sides (but which side?), to rationalize . . . and very inadequately. Sometimes an alien arm takes form outside his own arm, can no longer be dispelled or its growth arrested—an excess arm, exaggeratedly important, repetitive, proliferating into an "arm" world. "Re-arm." Super-arm, extension-arm, but of a meta-

6. Curiously, the emotions which suspend bodily sensations—"knees giving way" or "the heart stopped beating," for instance—leave no trace and scarcely any anxiety. This is owing to their short duration. The cognitive centers are not deeply or lastingly affected, beyond what one might call the acceptable limit of resilience. As often in madness, a threshold has to be crossed. These centers or these connections must have undergone not a shock, but a defeat.

mental extension, an extension which keeps coming back to mind, a second-growth arm, ubiquitous, metaphysical, ceaselessly yet uselessly renewed, an arm seized by perpetuation, a new sieve of the Danaïdes.

This arm which one could not stop feeling, whose extension mysteriously could not be arrested, will conversely break off at times, absurdly, at a third or quarter of its length; or will appear at a great distance, or oscillate between two or even more distances, or between two dimensions, two sizes. Somehow or other, the new arm is no longer coincident with the arm in front of one, uselessly before one (before one, like a proposal one can't agree to . . .).

On that day of distress (or exaltation) one learns what he would never have believed possible: that the sense of his body can be lost again with surprising ease.

Everyone can lose again the perception and spatial image of this body that took the infant so much effort and so many hundreds of days to acquire and construct, and of which the first drawings of children are the strange and simple evidence—one can lose this perception, this image, and in doing so find pleasure, horror, more often dejection.

At times, this may also happen without drugs.

As a result of senility, of initial sclerosis of cerebral arteries, of contusions, of the aftereffects of operations, of the shock of failure, of depression, of the menopause or (more rarely) the andropause, unfamiliar sensations bring into being, either insidiously or more often directly, a new inner shape, a new spatial image[7] of the body which, no

7. This happens in the case of hemiplegia, in certain lesions of the major and minor hemispheres of the brain. See H. Hécaen and J. de Ajuriaguerra, *op. cit.*

matter how disturbing and wrong it may be, must be faced up to—an image which somehow decamps from the body and rebuilds and refigures it. On the one hand, these sensations call the body into question, while on the other they make it provide the wrong answers,[8] which must be warded off, reinterpreted, eliminated. Generally the convalescent, once he is cured, does not sufficiently remember how confusing,[9] how troublesome[10] were these powerful sensations of burning, edema, swelling, inflammation of tissues, against which he had to struggle, at grips with agonies (and vainly, in delirium), persecuted by the eccentric sensations which stubbornly proposed and imposed an absurd self-configuration, an obsessive image that played no small part in his fever and his exhaustion.

It takes little enough to upset our architecture. Placing a simple tourniquet at arm level[11] disturbs the body's equilibrium, so that the subject's wrist, distorted and perverted in the mind, seems to have become a string or a peg.

---

8. See also "Les Illusions visuo-spatiales," P. Mouren and Tatossian, *L'Encéphale*, Vol. LII, 1963.

9. After an elbow fracture and the ensuing operation, which then entailed a post-traumatic osteoporosis, I had occasion, for days and nights, to observe in myself the intractable transformations of the affected limb which I experienced when my eyes were no longer open to watch it, and the force of this ceaseless pressure on the imagination. More recently, a simple broken finger enabled me to observe again the imperious changes, the changes *ad absurdum*, of the image of the body's structure in relation to the hand in question and also the development of this consciousness during convalescence. If for such a small matter the transformation experienced is great and imperative, how much more so in the case of a deep and serious lesion. Cf. "Bras cassé," *Tel Quel*, Spring 1962, no. 9.

10. Alajouanine, *Les Souffrances*, Paris.

11. An experiment by Meerovitch.

Though the hand has not moved it appeared as closed, lost, its fingers shortened or severed, the arm displaced . . .

But once the tourniquet is removed, everything is all right, restored to normal . . .

The disturbance caused by this loss—of the customary consciousness of a limb or even of a good half of the body—may be taken with a certain stoicism[12] by some patients who accept it the way they might accept other disturbances about which they can do nothing.

For others, who identify this loss with a feeling of insecurity, with worries, apprehensions, past terrors, this loss becomes unnerving, torturing. It nags them. It weighs upon them, cannot be tolerated, and gradually comes to disturb the entire person.

After sickness, accidents, prolonged suffering, a person may no longer be able to experience his body as before and may even be "sick of it" altogether. No longer does he feel at ease inside himself. The house of his body has been devalued. As though, having lost faith because of a limb he no longer feels or feels in the wrong way, he no longer wants to

12. The patient does not exaggerate his asymbolia to pain or his psychic blindness. And if he vainly searches for his ear under his shoulder and thinks he has found a third arm as he takes hold of his left one, if he loses touch with his entire left side, this does not necessarily become a crisis, an agonizing question which irresistibly impels him into delirium; instead it remains discreet, almost static. (Hécaen and J. de Ajuriaguerra, *op. cit.*; Angelergues and Hécaen, *La Cécité psychique*, and P. Angelergues, "Le Corps et ses images," in *L'Evolution psychiatrique*, no. 2, 1964.) This last study reports curious observations on not only the left side of the body, affected in certain diseases, but also on all space to the left which is affected, having ceased, partially at least, to matter.

return to his body. The body in which this or that part seems missing does not fill out again. The "lacunae" may change positions, but they no longer disappear. Suffering, lacunae, deficiencies are linked. At first there appeared between him and his body, because of the pain, an initial gap, for the physical pain one tries so hard to escape tends to alienation between him and his body; then new pains keep him from returning to it, from accepting it as such; apprehension combined with the experienced void has destroyed his confidence. The role of confidence is crucial: confidence is the function's double. To feel is to be disposed to feel, to accept feeling, to turn toward feeling, to have the certitude and the hope of feeling. Now he moves toward the void, toward absence. He encounters only himself. He who has once been seriously deceived in his body says that he has no organs left. He has detached himself from his body which, once having proved itself a traitor, he no longer dares trust, or resent. So he will abandon it, repudiate it. Though considering himself without a stomach, he nonetheless eats,[13] and the obvious corollary—that since he eats he must logically have a stomach—is insufficient to restore reality and effectively to counteract what is not felt. It is too late. Detachment and the persistent impression of "absence of organs" are fixed. The disease cannot be cured by reasoning; moreover, the subject is refractory to almost any treatment. He has become a hypochondriac.

The absence of a bodily sensation, or the newness of a strange metallic sensation, leads patients to believe that they have a zinc stomach, or that a coffer, some metallic apparatus, a compartment, a box, or a chest has taken its place. Or else it is their heart which is made out of aluminum or

---

13. Though sometimes, it is true, he must be forced to eat against his will.

lead. But always—as far as I can ascertain—there is at the outset a real physical illness, though sometimes almost totally forgotten, an accident, some suffering, and a momentary accidental perturbation of bodily awareness, with a discomfort that feeds a dim and dangerous apprehension.

Someone on a hunting party has been hit in the buttock by lead shot, pellets of which later turn up lower down, in his leg, or in his foot. And who knows where more shot may appear later? Someone else has been wounded in the shoulder by shrapnel, fragments of which have come out at the nape of the neck, in the neck itself, and at the shoulder; he fears that more will be found in other places, heaven only knows where. He does not feel "restored" to himself (and there may be a real difference, though he exaggerates it). It becomes crucial. A single, obsessive thought ensues, a raging desire to recover his absolute integrity;[14] hence his craving to be operated on at all costs and rid of this strange thing which has replaced his normal body.

Another person has had nothing more serious than a sore throat, a cauterization, a minor operation, a tonsillectomy. Subsequently, the disease spreads. His internal, anguished attention spreads. He is ready for any sort of intervention to be rid of it. He expects from surgery what he could not obtain from his own mind. A deserter from his body, he begs. He is helpless, hysterical. A medicine which as side effect causes some dryness of the mucous membranes, or an

14. One must not question the body's diagram too closely. It will answer with gaps and mistakes. It is somewhat vague. And even to a healthy man, it will not afford the correct answers he expects. As soon as one tries, eyes closed, without moving, to feel it, to reconstitute it, the body turns out to be less than solid. Apprehension instantly undoes it. More virtual than real, it is when it seems missing that one is conscious that the body had some kind of shape.

aversion to food, is a new trauma for him, the starting point of a new fear, the fear of new damage to an organ, etc. The hypochondria proliferates.[15]

Actually, sickness reveals a previously unrealized attachment to the body and a narcissism without which[16] his hypochondria, it appears, would not be possible.

In such a case, a measure of participation, of hysteria, is involved; it becomes a kind of appreciable distinction to have been on an operating table twenty times. More often, the subject bemoans the fact, utterly depressed.

Another person, with paranoid tendencies, upset by the sense of loss or displacement of organs, accuses a surgeon of having removed his stomach, or his heart, and of having put machinery in its place. He threatens, seeking to restore justice by the mortal revenge he is contemplating.

Contrary to what often happens to an amputee who has the illusion of a "ghost limb" (where the misleading sensation remains quite stable and fixed, the amputated arm, for example, being still felt, with its wrist watch), an illusion which appears[17] "as the repressed experience of a former present which cannot bring itself to become past," the hypochondriac's disease[18] strikes suddenly, dramatically,

15. And if centers of co-ordination exist, they will have suffered irrecoverable damage.
16. Paul Schilder, *The Image and Appearance of the Human Body*, New York, 1958.
17. According to Maurice Merleau-Ponty.
18. We must return to this sense of abstraction. The healthy man does not easily reach the point of imagining that someone may lose his body, that, without being dead or having undergone an amputation, he may find himself with nothing.
The drug experience is essential in shedding light on this matter. R. B., a friend who twice tried hashish without much pleasure, recently reminded me of his first impression, which was of being suddenly bodyless—his body spirited away. He could

and virtually always is ready to turn into something else, to assume a new, dangerous, and alarming form.

In losing the sense of the body, one is also prepared to lose the sense of its limits.

One transforms one's own body into another body, into that of another person, of an animal, of a demon, into a large urban mass.

An abstraction, a transformation, a hugeness of the body which almost nothing can ever stop or limit.

No longer can it be restrained, no longer arrested. It transforms and extends itself in responding to its discomforts, images, reflections.

Released from the measure and restriction[19] the body imposes as long as one is conscious of it, released from what keeps one's "incorporated" being compact, the subject "sees big," he sees enormous. He may feel that a barracks could be lodged within his body, or an entire city. No specific dimension presents difficulties, provided that it is considerable.

A huge extension is experienced. A workman, hitherto modest, feels he has grown to a nameless, gigantic size. He is afraid that if he falls he will smother the crowd, destroy the city and its outlying regions, crack the earth. He fears that if he urinates he will flood[20] the world and tries to

---

not get over his amazement at what seemed a magician's trick. He remained bodiless for hours. "I was hollow," he told me, "truly hollow, a hollow statue." He was disconcerted to notice that he had no pulse. It seemed that he had no heart left. (An impression often recorded in psychiatric medicine, notably in the case of general paralysis, if we look up early observations.)

19. Delirium of vastness. The Cottard Syndrome.

20. If the experimenters were less prudish and cared more for truth than appearances, we should have known long ago and by many examples that this is precisely one of the impressions mescaline produces—having imbibed a good deal of the sweetened

prevent such a disaster by efforts to control his bladder.

Apprehension is nothing new to these giants.

Concomitant with the abstraction of the body, there is an impression familiar to dozens and hundreds of unsuspecting, dumfounded mescaline experimenters, which has its equivalents in several mental illnesses and ranges far into unreality and megalomania—the impression of a current, of an unending flow.

An impression of endless prolongation, of infinite extension, of perpetuity, of immortality, from which minds quick to philosophize and rediscover their hidden desires return with peremptory metaphysical convictions.

Just as there exists a certain banality in the imaginary "visions" of the world of drugs, as well as a certain banality in the illusory sensations, there also exists a certain metaphysical banality consisting of the common human basis of thought that instantly transmutes itself into beliefs bearing on Immensity, Eternity, Immortality. The Absolute. Immanence. What is beyond Time, Space, the accidental, the phenomenal.

The impression of Immateriality engenders them.

It is in the schizophrenic state that the "immeasurable" is most disturbing, most damaging.

The vastness perceived by some[21] was still part of reality, a baroque implantation in reality, an excess within the finite. Such vastness was not without a certain limit.

---

liquid, one has the strange, unique, and laughable impression, though it is anything but funny at the time, that if one yields to a certain need, one will flood the world. (An impression consisting simultaneously of vastness, limitlessness in space, and endlessness in time.)

21. In the Cottard Syndrome.

Here it is an entirely different matter—a more complete dissipation of the finite, on several levels, a breakup of time, space, and the functions and arrangements which sustain the world, other people, and one's "ego" itself.

A metaphysical dispossession takes the place of a simple abstraction of the body.

"Everything is limitless," says the schizophrenic.[22] "Another sky, black and terrifying, is behind the real sky of an autumn evening."

"Space seems to be receding, expanding to infinity. I feel myself surrendered to an infinitely large space. The old space detaches itself from this other space like a ghost," says another. "Everything is limitless."

Hundreds of so-called schizophrenics, thousands of others as yet uncategorized, who were uprooted from themselves and their surroundings by a dose of mescaline, have used the same words, have known the same boundlessness, the same dispersion of their own bounds, the same fading of relations with what is limited, pragmatic, and with the strange limited beings who are other men, chattering on, unknowing, without any suspicion of the other universe.

No longer does one reach fixed bounds, limitations. Whatever one does, one is in the endless waves of the boundless.

In a way, this is something of a regression.

The child at its earliest age identified hand, head, breast, the mother and himself in a spherical, spherifying, global impression, with no beginning or end. Only sleep, recurring often, returned to surround them, but is sleep a boundary?

What a strange planet each of us has been. Man is a child

22. In Fischer, quoted by Mouren and Tatossian, *op. cit.*, and many other examples, notably in Jaspers, Bleuler, Henri Ey, Minkowski, and throughout psychiatric literature.

who has spent a lifetime confining, limiting, testing himself, seeing himself as limited, accepting himself as limited. As an adult he has succeeded, almost succeeded.

Whatever he says or does, Infinity is something every man responds to, something fundamental. It reminds him of something. This is where he comes from . . .

That is why Infinity, taught to the child somewhat later, but still in his early years, "takes" so well. He offers little resistance to the infinite god inculcated in him in most civilizations at a time when he was virtually defenseless; a belief, which henceforth becomes second nature, is taken for granted, self-evident, a conviction for which he will do battle if need be.

Yet the schizophrenic rarely regains his religion, and almost never in distressed states. Religion was also a kind of localization, a one-way street, a dam to keep Infinity blocked up, in its place.

He who finds himself, as a result of treacherous chemistry in his body, in an exceptional state, in a Beyond that is beyond religions, beyond all superstructures, symbolisms, intermediaries (angels or saints and of course priests and sacerdotal representatives), is lost in an infinitely deranging Infinity; an Infinity allowing for no return (unlike the Infinity of meditation, which, once the hour of concentrated meditation is past, complacently returns to the comfortable nest of the finite), unlike the Infinity of the theologian who gives a lecture on it and then goes back home again; no—a dead-end Infinity, which does not permit any return to the finite, the definite, the contours of the definite, of the definable, of the definitive, a treacherous Infinity which makes anything finite inaccessible: the self, the world, and other men. That man does not regain his religion.

The schizophrenic is alone. without defensible borders.

Behind every entity there is a world. No organized unit subsists. His state has reduced it to dust.

The infinitization, the perpetuation, the atomization, the undifferentiated fragmentation, aggravated by the antagonistic and conflicting agitation which reduces everything to absurdity, permits nothing but ambivalence, reiterations, obstinacy, refusal, and an inhuman detachment.

This is the only possible attitude to be taken by someone in whom everything is atomized, "disconnected," "dissident," who is broken by the impossibility of "feeling together," of "imagining together," or "reasoning together," and for whom the body, the "person," the "other," the "real," concordance and convergence are inaccessible.[23]

23. What he feels is not nothing, but it cannot be co-ordinated, cannot be expressed. An exasperating state, since those around you understand nothing, always guess wrong, and are satisfied with it. The schizophrenic, habitually withdrawn inside himself, in sudden exasperation explodes against his parents whom he hates, trivial, sentimental family figures who comprehend nothing, and intuit nothing, checked forever on their ridiculous level.

Adolescent schizophrenics often reveal themselves by a deep hatred of their parents, those "sensitive people" around them who do not "feel" them.

VII. THE NEED TO OVERLOAD AND TO DE-SIMPLIFY

The state in which we see the schizophrenic conceals many things which, very fragmentarily, intermittently, and very ineffectively, he discovers only for himself, and which he could not, even if he wished, reveal to others.

His is an inexpressible, disorganizing universe, to which others have no access and which forces him to withdraw into himself, refusing all communication. Very little of this singularity which inhabits him is evident to others.

In spite of being shut up in himself, one or the other may, in devious hermetic form, express the marvelous, singular world of which outsiders have no notion and which makes the false no falser than the "truth" of others. His gestures in particular, sketched rather than accomplished, their general quality, his manner of someone who knows more than he is telling, his expression of innuendo, of mystery, afford no clue. He knows something others[1] do not know. He moves where others do not venture.

In other words, more profoundly than any other human

1. All others. One schizophrenic does not comprehend another.

being, he feels that nothing is simple or happens simply, that everything is complex, irremediably divergent, contradictory.

Seeing him in this state, psychiatrists, speaking for those who are normal, say he is "mannered."

"Mannerism," Hermann Minkowski writes, "refers to the mannered man we prefer to see simpler, more direct, more immediate, not only in his gestures, in his movements, but in his way of thinking, of feeling."

But such simplicity has no meaning for the schizophrenic —it does not suit him, it seems inadequate, artificial, inappropriate.

His gestures, his signs (in his "elaborate" drawings), show that he shuns it.

In his state, it is an insane multiplicity which is natural and simplicity which is unnatural, crude, beside the point, insipid.

Even in his writing—which some authorities[2] also call mannered—he shuns this simplicity. Mannered or not, it needs to be observed closely. Spelling, vocabulary, meaning, syntax, and handwriting as well are often peculiar. Recalcitrant to simplicity and to rules, the schizophrenic has introduced his own emphases and diacritical signs, each independent of the rest, at each of the different levels of language. At the level of vocabulary he employs neologisms; at the level of spelling, repetition—letters or syllables are repeated two and three times; at the level of handwriting, spirals, curlicues on letters, inordinate underlinings; at the semantic level, hermeticism—exaggerated, indecipherable ellipses, obvious solecisms.

The text, thus crammed with underlined though disparate

2. By Bleuler first. More recently by Henri Maurel, "Le maniérisme du langage," *Entretiens psychiatriques 5*, Presses Universitaires de France, 1960.

signs which do not operate synergetically, fails to constitute a meaningful whole.

The author of the text does not seem to see it as a whole, nor, in particular, to imagine the effect which his letter, when he writes one, drafted in this manner, with its discordant elements, will produce on others. What he has laboriously underlined will single him out not as a remarkable man but as a man unaware of the total effect, unable to control it, a man from whom the text escapes altogether.

In many other areas as well appears the tormenting need for de-simplification.

One day, passing through the corridors of a provincial psychiatric hospital, I happened upon a most astonishing table.

Once noticed, it continued to occupy one's mind. It even persisted, as it were, in going about its own business, as though the table or its maker, still undecided, were still debating whether it would be a table or something else. "A typical example of objectified mannerism," remarked the specialist accompanying me.

Mannered—this table, the heaviest, densest imaginable?

True, it was a long way from being quite simply a table, the way other tables are.

The striking thing was that it was neither simple nor really complex, initially or intentionally complex, or constructed according to a complicated plan. Instead, it had been de-simplified in the course of its carpentering.

Slow at his work, sedulous, a perfectionist (when for example he had to "clean up" a room, he spent three days scouring everything, polishing the floor, making what would soon be carelessly soiled sparkle with an ideal cleanliness), its creator, E., had taken more than a year to finish it, or rather to bring it to its present state, for was it really finished? As it stood, it was a table of additions, much like certain schizophrenics' drawings, described as "overstuffed,"[3] and if finished it was so only in so far as there was no way of adding anything more to it, the table having become more and more an accumulation, less and less a table.

An increasingly compact aggregate, this was the work of someone who periodically returns to the idea of a "table." For it had not been made haphazardly, either. The most important phenomenon had occurred in time. The table before us was the result of continual manipulation. Its creator never stopped reworking it, complicating it, "overstuffing" it.

By repeatedly inserting, quite ingenuously, little blocks, useless additions, supplements to supplements—the sign of an irresistible tendency to elaborate without ever being able to stop, without ever considering his work as "finished"—E. had toiled on in the direction of "table." Had he produced one? It was not intended for any specific purpose, for anything one expects of a table. Heavy, cumbersome, it was virtually immovable. One didn't know how to handle it (mentally or physically). Its top surface, the useful part of the table, having been gradually reduced, was disappearing, with so little relation to the clumsy framework that the thing did not strike one as a table, but as some freak piece of furniture, an unfamiliar instrument . . . for which there was no purpose. A dehumanized table, nothing cozy about it, nothing "middle class," nothing rustic, nothing countrified, not a kitchen table or a work table. A table which lent itself to no function, self-protective, denying itself to service and communication alike.

There was something stunned about it, something petri-

3. *Bourré*; the expression is Dr. G. Ferdière's.

fied. Perhaps it suggested a stalled engine. Someone to whom a photograph was shown made this remark, knowing nothing about the artisan. Although since his arrival at the asylum E. had been employed only as a sort of domestic, a job at which he proved to be extremely confident and careful though very slow, he had previously been a truck driver, an occupation which had doubtless obliged him on more than one occasion, when his truck had broken down on the highway, to take a look at the engine under the hood—an engine which therefore may bear some analogy to this complicated, enigmatic table, it too stalled like E.'s life now, something in his own head inexplicably blocked, a deranged brain which does not yield its secret.

The table in question had never been used. It had doubtless never occurred to anyone to use it as a table. During a later visit we paid to E., we saw in the corridor another table he had made, close to some workmen who were making minor repairs; nothing had been placed on it, although there were tools and boards and scraps of wood lying around, which it would have been much easier to pick up from the table than from the floor. Had E. forbidden using it? It appeared, rather, that this table embodied its own *ban*, a bizarre object whose understanding and use required initiation and which, "burdened with itself," seemed to reject any further burden, and whose scheme of organization, alien to familiar ideas, kept it at a distance.

Needless to say, tables as such constituted no problem for E. He used those of the asylum which had no particular character of their own.

But the natural state of a simple table was insufficient for him[4] when it came to making one.

4. After my first mescaline experiment, I remember how I felt the urge to draw curlicues, spirals, zigzags, how I filled page after page with them and certainly not out of any predilec-

Similarly, another inmate is not satisfied with the natural state of the word "palliative" which he will write pallillillliattivetive, although he recognizes the word without hesitation in the text or the newspaper he is reading, and sees that it is written with only one "t," only two "ll's," only one "tive," and without that enormous curlicue he has added to the "p." But he needs this redoubling, he is driven by an expansion of sorts inside him (despite a coldness and a distinct cessation of sociability), he is driven by *palliative* to go beyond.

The rules of language, even if he often transgresses them, more often also keep him nonetheless enslaved.

It is by drawing or coloring or painting that he may, even if he had never drawn or painted before, at last be able to give himself (in part by giving himself up) to the conflicting multiplicity which so binds and bothers him, to the hallucinations which torment him, and to the proliferation—especially to the proliferation—to the repetitions, to the extravagance of repetitions, yielding, able at last to yield to the extreme eagerness of repetition which possesses him.

E., the creator of the table, had other modes of expression.

His greetings, particularly when he caught sight of a

---

tion for ornamentation, which is not one of my talents. This scribbling all slanted in the same direction. I remember even more vividly the next day looking in bookshop windows at reproductions of masterpieces of the finest periods, which at the time seemed to me insufferably simple, even silly. Nothing in me corresponded to them any longer.

sympathetic nurse or an intern he knew, formed an extravagant sequence. As though an ordinary greeting were evidently inadequate, he composed a kind of festival of welcome, a whole pantomime of gestures expressing approbation and delight, as well as playfulness, banter, resistance, flourishes—a masterpiece of complication and mumbo-jumbo. A veritable ritual, mocking, enigmatic, with perhaps a touch of defiance about it, a hidden challenge.

This impression stayed with me, though what I saw was neither as complex nor as agitated as at first. The impulse and its converse, that is, several small corrective impulses which inevitably followed, sapping all confidence, struck me by their asymmetrical ambivalence. The difficult speech which followed, discontinuous, sometimes hurried, stammering, seemed to try, with ordinary words first put forth and then withdrawn, to utter the inexpressible and then to erase it.

E. was presenting a show, a show of welcome. But it was an overly explosive show, followed by a circumspect, embarrassing withdrawal. Quick, fierce, defiant glances, vanishing as soon as they appeared—merciless glances shot from his eyes. I saw in them a potential of rage, destruction, a terrible immediacy capable of sweeping everything before it. Since this was not overly apparent, he was indulged at the asylum, did work provided he wasn't asked to do too much and was allowed to do the job in his own way. To my way of feeling, an irreducible "something" was always present.

Twenty years ago, he had killed his wife, savagely. He had done away with her. Done away with a source of aggravation. He had been removed from society for good, nor did he care to return to it, not even for a day or two. When a physician, in my presence, proposed a day's "leave," he was not tempted, but nearly gave way to panic. His expression became that of a hunted man. Outside, how quickly everything becomes complicated, irritating, and one cannot always control oneself.

To return to E.'s table: it touched occasional visitors rather than shocked them as the apparently chaotic work of some modern artist would have done, for all its unity of insolence, daring, and skill. They wondered what kind of incompetent could not even manage to make a table.

As a matter of fact, unconcerned by his materials and their unfortunate effect on the whole, E. had used, for example, old pieces of worn linoleum to match the wooden parts here and there.

Yet the most touching thing was that although he periodically returned to symmetry, as though to an obligation, nonetheless the parts did not harmonize. Zeal had not sufficed to make them harmonize.

His disharmony (an early term for schizophrenia was the disease of disharmonies) had got the upper hand.

VIII. EXPERIMENTAL ALIENATIONS

A.

In performing an alienating experiment upon oneself, it is crucial that enough alertness be maintained to observe the ill-used mind[1] which, continuously active, tries to carry on its functions, proceeding differently, disparately, leading down strange paths.

Virtually without realizing it, one finds oneself, by oblique, deviating processes, which almost infallibly follow an initial anxiety, deceived, incapable of correcting error, ineffectual. Here, among many others, are some models of such defective sequences, processes which, it would seem, do not differ greatly from what goes on in many (unprovoked) mental illnesses. Here then are various points of departure, developments, conclusions.

1. *The Starting Point: A diffuse, internal excitation*, at first, only slight, then developing, a limitless excitation whose source is imperceptible . . . as well as its objective,

1. For this, appropriate—i.e., minimum—doses of the most commonly known hallucinogens have generally been used.

which is neither noise, sound, color, light, thought, nor anything of the kind, yet which can become many things, an enormous number of things—an augmentation, a dim augmentation, already a presence, soon a crowd.

Possible consequences: The impression grows; one hears, when there is nothing to hear, a "brr" which will become *a rustling*, a dull, hence distant murmur which increases, hence of something which must have drawn nearer, which must be guarded against, hence a threat, a danger, a danger which does not show up as it should, which does not reveal itself as anything recognizable, which remains imperceptible, unfamiliar, enigmatic, suspicious;[2] which resembles murmurs, faint recriminations, voices, voices which cannot be localized.

2. *The Starting Point:* Always this infinitesimal, *immanent, intrapsychic agitation,* an imperceptible movement like that of a vibrating metallic plate, yet the very soul of one's being has passed into these vibrations.

Consequence: The surroundings seem similarly affected. It becomes difficult, even with an effort, to tell if inert

2. One is surrounded by a generalized noise. One hears a noise like the approach of a marching army or a truck drawing near. One hears the noise of the steady beat of a motor as if a locomotive were nearby, an indefinable, dull, powerful, alarming noise, hitherto unknown. The amplified noises, shifted by an unfamiliar perception, turn the dim sound of the blood in the cerebral arteries into a deep murmur which seems to have come from outside, from far away.

The heart (its beating amplified very distinctly—though this phenomenon is not always realized) gives the illusion of a factory, of rhythmic marching, of a two-piston motor. The clenched jaws elicit—a procession.

things might not be alive, alive with a cunning hidden life, an intra-life similar to that life which we sense *beneath* our own. The *hiatus* between the animate and the inanimate is no longer apparent. One's agitation radiates, expands.

The inanimate has ceased being far from the animate. Made dynamic, capable of movement, the source of movements, everything everywhere seems ready to become animate.

The mineral kingdom no longer has its old weighty and restful solidity. Every object is charged, is potential.[3] Whether made of wood, stone, leather, or any other material, it has lost its dense and stable look. A truly static state is no longer imaginable.

Hence many initial illusions where the object seems about to move.

Under these conditions, remaining still or calm would not be natural: one is no longer safe. Fear may come, if for some reason it is not already there.

3. *The Starting Point: An impression of floating in one's body*, with which one no longer coincides, which one no longer occupies fully, vigorously, satisfactorily.

One is no longer protected by its (absent) will, by its (lost) self-control, by its (vanished) ease in shifting position, directing and moving itself.

Without supposing himself hunted, one has already the same sensation as a man who is really hunted.

One possible consequence will be that one no longer feels secure. Anxiety sets in. One wonders if someone might not take advantage of this condition. One expects to be ob-

3. Hallucinations or illusions of the same sort: a stuffed lizard will seem alive, ready to scurry away, but a live lizard, if motionless, will not seem stuffed.

served, criticized, mocked . . . In apprehension, one comes to seek where the persecution will come from.

Mistrust sets in.

4. *The Starting Point:* The impression of no longer being in command of all one's powers. (Which is true.)

Consequence: A certain loss of authority, reminiscent to some people of childhood, the state in which authority was other people (father, teachers, judges, watchmen, police).

During the initial period of life, a long-lasting habit is being established: the fear of being reprimanded. For often unfathomable reasons, one risks being reprimanded for a large number of acts (a deplorable abstraction makes such acts "reprehensible" in themselves). In childhood, a habit is established that makes one see, beyond and instead of one's own view, the point of view of the grownups—those fearsome, censorious people with the power to reprimand, beat, punish, accuse, etc. The adult's achievement—to be no longer, or no longer in quite this way, liable to punishment—is undone with the unsettling return of insecurity and the loss of self-mastery, which recalls and resuscitates the ancient childhood estate of dependence, of non-autonomy. It is other people who are once again the masters, the powerful, the tyrants, the persecutors.

It may also suggest the feeling of guilt when, uncertain whether or not one would be punished or reprimanded, one appeared before the tribunal of the father, the principal, the teacher.

5. *The Starting Point:* As one is no longer located as before in one's body, the impression arises of having become *a kind of free spirit.*

Detached.
Vibrating on another psychic level.

Consequence: The impression of being, instead of a body, *a psychic being,* causes one to expect psychic presences as well (it is later that they appear as physical). One has the impression of presences, one feels variations of presences, reinforcements of presences, of half-presences. Behind one, beside one, in shadowy places, but in the light as well, in corners, in recesses, one feels, one sees presences coming, already there are infra-presences, dense voids on the way to becoming presences. Out of space, charged like oneself, emerges a threat of being. Apparitions will follow, but it is the state previous to the apparition which matters, the potential apparition[4] everywhere possible, everywhere capable of rising up, of increasingly manifesting itself. *That* is the phenomenon.

Consequence: Invasion by presences.[5] Presences of this order make no "entry." They are there, and one's territory is invaded. The kind of antechamber each of us possesses, which permits one to keep someone nearby at a distance, no longer functions. No more antechamber. The other person

---

4. Fear and apprehension are by no means inevitable. One may even discover many presences which are marvelous or even agreeable, or merely embarrassing.

5. People with no understanding of apparitions ask for details of shape and manner of dress. This is not what matters, except it is true, for some women, even saints, who do not discard the habit of considering attire. What matters is that someone is there who should not be there.

When there is an apparition, participation—the relation with the appearing figure—takes over, even if one says nothing and thinks little. You become part of a whole. This consciousness fills the mind. An observation that is also valid for illusions.

enters you. He violates your vital space. The glances[6] of others are cast upon you without filtering.

One is vulnerable, open to being traumatized, the threshold of suffering is instantly reached.

The presence of certain people becomes unbearable. Certain glances, even in photographs, strike a defenseless self.

Loss of psychic territory, of ownership of one's ground.

Ground reduced to little more than a point.

Impression of the other person's presence, of his pressure, of his encroachment. The other person experienced as a threat, as an attacker, as a pursuer, attempting to act upon oneself.

You cannot look at someone without feeling a relatedness. You are looked at and feel the weight, the new, excessive weight of the glances which concern you, supposedly, even if these glances are vague, cast in passing.

You feel watched: if you feel guilty about something, the two feelings converge, leading to catastrophe.

6. *The Starting Point: A feeling of expansion*, of uncontrollable expansion, which spreads and persists, inundating, radiating, oceanic, which will break like waves, which must break, which tries to swarm, a pullulation, a maximum, beyond the maximum, extreme, yet constantly increased by new surges.

A state of seething. Something of extreme importance has to be declared, to be proclaimed to the entire world, with the utmost urgency.

The consequences are familiar: thus dilated, one feels,

6. Hence a reaction in many mentally ill persons who attack the eyes. In the past, many accidents were caused in this way.

one declares oneself extremely important, important beyond anything. If this state should persist, there comes a compulsion to call oneself Ruler, Emperor, God.

The expansion continues. Often there develops simultaneously the *impression of tension,* as if one were a violin string being pressed harder, increasingly harder, incredibly harder, yet not to the breaking point. One would like to cry for mercy, if only there were someone able to grant mercy, able to break the intolerable tension.

A tension which must be broken. At all costs.

Unable to resist any longer, some people commit suicide for no special reason other than that something *must stop.*

They cannot see beyond, and their life, too, stops; though this instinctive consequence may not have been actually foreseen.

Raptus, sudden impulses take hold: actions are committed before being considered, even actions of the most extreme kind—murder, suicide, arson, destruction . . . matching the inner fury. Thought, short-circuited, has been left behind.

At another level of self, you no longer hold yourself back. You no longer hold back. You release the secrets. The secrets[7] that ought to have been most closely kept.

---

7. Under the effects of the alienating excitation of peyotl, the natives of Mexico, according to the old Spanish chronicles, could no longer keep their secrets.

The readiness to speak, to betray oneself, to confess, induced by hallucinogens (of which psylocybin is one) is made use of by psychiatrists who administer such drugs to mental patients, causing them to speak at last and confess what they have hitherto managed to keep hidden.

The insane also reveal their secrets (in words or in drawings) directly or symbolically . . . though greatly altered. One has therefore to beware of deducing from the content of an insane mind a norm and model for the nature of the nonalienated per-

They rise to the lips, one is busy speaking even before realizing that a secret is being betrayed.

7. *The Starting Point:* Now everything presses too heavily, *weighs,* penetrates.

Wounds, ugliness, accidents, scuffles, the sight of an open maw, a skull, a hoof, no longer are sights like any others, or merely informative; they have become painful, alarming—

---

son's secret thought. For instance, madness, even though highly erotic in its expressions, does not indicate that erotic preoccupation is the constant of a lifetime and the stuff accumulated in the subconscious; nor are the insane identifying with God the Father indicative of the normal preoccupation with the Infinite or of the actual content of the normal subconscious. Not at all—but madness is most at home in erotization and divinization. It is an altogether different thing.

Importance of restraints: "At the age of three," states one psychiatric manual (Gillespie's), "most children have succeeded in controlling their bladder, both in daytime and at night."

This modest success has an enormous importance for the future adult—and failure an even greater importance; he will not easily recover from it, and perhaps never entirely. The first defeat is felt as shameful. It is the first betrayal of oneself, the visible sign of a hidden weakness designating a weak point, that of control.

It is notable that in psychiatry the sphincteral deficiency of children should be regarded as so serious, alarming, significant. In primitive societies, a boy, in order to gain access to the company of men, must habitually give evidence of his aptitude for control. Initiation often consists of the submission to pain without crying out, suffering with control of suffering. A suffering which is to be kept hidden. An adult is someone who can keep a secret. Then he is admitted among men, who will divulge to him the secrets of men, secrets which cannot be divulged to children or to women. Inured, he will be able to be a warrior on whom the tribe can count . . . who will not betray. Secrets, mental sphincters, which retain what must be retained.

In certain professions, the man who is not a man, the man unworthy of manhood, is not the killer but the man whom one cannot trust, the potential traitor.

they echo, persist, unbalance. One must be careful to avoid them. State of vigilance.

Consequence: Appearance of harm. Contrary to what happens in the normal state, where perception is moderated and "filtered," the same things perceived in this new state erupt violently, do harm, and do not go away.

Sensation quickly attains the threshold of pain.

Life, now, is Invasion. One lives under an occupation.

8. *The Starting Point: Another invasion, from within.* Evocations, fragments of memories, impressions, images, sounds, return in force.

What should be attenuated, like something heard long ago and forgotten, comes back. Imaginary noises are perceived as if they were real. It is extremely difficult to tell the difference, which is not the one that might be expected. Even if the hallucinatory sound is faint, it is more momentous, more undeniable than a real noise . . .[8] In this case, one might be advised, all that is needed is not to believe in it. But the hallucinatory noise is always a perfectly believ-

8. One day, when I was listening to the illusory, hallucinatory sound of an oboe, some children came out of the suddenly opened door of the apartment downstairs and began pounding on wooden slats. The noise established in my mind did not conflict with *their* noises, *their* music.

Of course, one hampered the other, but not as if they both came from outside. No, my oboe was on a different level, an interior level. *Their* noises, loud as they were, were superficial, and on "my" periphery, merely trying to enter. Of course children's shouts are shrill and their noises drowned out everything. Yet, they did not interfere with that of the oboe.

The oboe was the inhabitant, endowed with a full, rich life; the others were "proposed" noises. I had never noticed so clearly how, to my great astonishment, a real sound, though loud, can be insignificant, transitory, external, inadequate, and, for all its uproar, more questionable than the hallucinatory sound.

able one, more believable than perceived. A genuinely perceived noise is less absorbing.

9. *The Starting Point:* Objects that had never been anything but ordinary, people too, pictures, portraits seem charged with emphatic, bothersome, unpleasant, suspect meanings.

It is true that every object normally has one and several meanings. It has a purpose. It has a meaning. It was meant for something. An intention has brought it here. An endeavor which we reconstruct approximately and rapidly, if need be, by means of interpretation.

Interpretation, a large subject which must be taken up again and again, which must be dealt with at some length, which does not proceed of its own accord; far from it.

Now, *within it, meanings seethe.*

Tentative interpretations. Many bad ones for each good one. Every object seems ready to reveal and mean things, many things—unexpected, surprising, yet indubitable things.

No longer are there any objects that remain totally neutral—any objects which one is sure will remain totally neutral, without affording new horizons.

10. *The Starting Point:* Like certain sensations, certain ideas, for no apparent reason, take up too much space.

One can no longer get rid of them—they have become viscous, catching, insistent, fascinating, prevalent . . . in a way that no longer permits consideration of any others.

Consequence: Is this what it means to be *autosuggestionable?* One has become *obedient to certain ideas,* whose uncommon, unjustified scope blocks the horizon. One's secret, objectless exaltation, once it encounters an interesting object or idea, begins reworking it, dismantling it, taking it to such extremes that it becomes absurd.

The danger of evocations which become impregnations.

Imagining something causes one to experience it as though it were real. In a short time, the true reality is discredited by comparison.

Just as one's consciousness in a drug experience devalues normal consciousness, madness, whether provoked or not, discredits the normal state of mental health.

A tendency to scoff.

11. *The Starting Point: The difficulty* of compartmentalizing, of *defining,* of attributing to each person, each object, idea, action, what is proper to it. *One no longer sees what is proper to it,* what is its own.

In his normal state, there is in man a constant procession of thoughts—contrasting, opposing, contradicting thoughts —followed by new thoughts that support the first, interrupted by a thought remote from the first ones and, at least for some moments, leading away from them, then returning.

This is the basis on which we perform mental operations. The human race is given to hold on to its own.

Which operation? As the first idea arises and is accepted, we attribute it to ourselves; equally the next one of the same type. We acknowledge it as our own. The subsequent opposing ones we then commonly attribute to an imaginary, convenient opponent. This simplifies matters. But it is probably an automatic opposition, held by no one in particular. As for the interloper leading out of the field, we treat it as though we had *wanted* it for comparison's sake, whereas in all likelihood nothing of the kind is the case. The idea has arisen by itself and we, running after it, seek to appropriate it in this way.

The state of sanity, like all the states of the righteous, is a state of convenience and hypocrisy, not of integrity. The mentally sane individual supports, in the mind's flux, certain ideas; those he rejects he attributes to others. Ideas become props for much "discrimination"—held on the one hand and repudiated on the other. Whereas the man who is mentally ill lets things slide—he does not take hold. His attributions of qualities, his determinations—if he makes them—are, because of his difficulties, approximate, maladjusted.

Consequence: Elimination of the person in charge—observant, attentive, bent on effectiveness; the focus of ideas no longer exists, nor their precise application. It existed only by virtue of an operation of supervision, of control, of constraint. Only by this means could it be sustained.

Discontinuities will continue to occur. But with the sequence observed and tested, they will end up by being known and understood.

Mental illnesses under observation reveal only a small portion of possible mental disturbances.

One might, and surely will, invent other disturbances of the mind, causing well-defined, circumscribed damage, as well as new, extensive disintegrations, to give scope to sophisticated observation. These experiments will reveal the natural forms of madness, hitherto examined, to be, by comparison, clumsy, crude, and confused aggregations.

A mental disorganization planned in precise detail is yet

to be achieved. It will be the role of chemistry above all, and of a selective electric cerebral excitation, to provoke, to detect, to distinguish, to isolate from one another the multiple factors which give the illusion of one *and which, in fact, are a "group."*

In this way, one will be able to follow to its end, to its consequences, its maximum extension, a root of disturbances.

B. The Unexplained Immensity

Rereading what I have written, I notice how much I have shown or tried to show of the intelligible.

In doing so, I was misleading the reader.

Assailed in the course of tumultuous experiences, assailed in outbursts and avalanches by the incomprehensible, I should have been, I suppose, content to accept the challenge and to find, all the same, something intelligible in these states inundated by the absurd and the ineffable. Under the downpour of insanities, and continually losing my grip, I was determined to hold on to whatever could possibly be grasped, however inadequately, however fragmentarily. I clung.

Too much. I went too far.

It is high time I made it known. Three or four facts will suffice, restoring to its very modest place the meager "known" amid the immensity that is still unknown.

First of all, I have rarely been fully aware throughout an entire experiment, from beginning to end.

The middle part largely escaped me. "I" faded into it. I

lack many "middles," while I retain almost all the beginnings. Most last parts are also missing. At the end, the end which is peace regained, a great, incomparable peace, one no longer has the same kind of awareness. One is no longer entirely sure that being aware is a good idea.

As a result, there are enormous gaps. I would follow, yes, but fascinated, obtuse. If someone were to give a false description of these extraordinary vanished parts, I would be able to say "No, that is not it." My knowledge of many points, even important points which I experienced, ends about there.

Another fact:
Concerning the visions: for many hours I have had interior visions. Thousands of scenes passed by, torrents of images. I followed astounded, exalted, then I lost my footing. Only barely and with great difficulty could I grasp what the first ones, the first four or five visions, signified and how they were evoked. Beyond that, up to perhaps eight or nine images, comprehending them was a matter of luck. Then, I no longer perceived the link between associations, I saw no reason why one should be connected to another, the ninth to the tenth, the eleventh to the twelfth image (or scene). There was no longer any track. Everything diverged more and more.

Sometimes, just as a fortuitously interrupted dream reveals its connections and its relations, it might happen that after an interruption of several sequences, I would grasp again (to a degree) the reason for such and such a scene, but at once the senseless, "hypersensed" procession resumed, quite beyond the grasp of my understanding.

There may be persons who will think I did not try hard enough. Convinced of the existence of a subconscious where obsessions, complexes, subjects of frustration, memories, and repressed painful scenes lie dormant, ready to awaken, they imagine that these obsessive images come again to life, more or less as they used to be, appearing and reappearing compulsively. However, no such recurrence is discernible.

One of the first "observers" of the effects of hashish reports that during a session of ten hours' duration or more, an image occurs only once, does not recur, never repeats itself (an observation so generally true and accurate that it might be called Ludlow's Law[9]).

The images are of an inexhaustible newness. One cannot count on their return to reflect upon them, understand them. Wherein they certainly differ from dreams.

Another fact:

When I was in a reflective mood, when reflections came to me, one after another, it happened that after some time spent in abstract thought one such reflection hooked up to an image. At this moment I perceived the interrelation, the first image being a sort of model, the following a comparison, then a third appeared, and a fourth, a fifth . . . images always, associations surely, but digressions as much as parallels. They passed, not so as to lead but to mislead through endless diversifications, each one being a break or a leap increasingly difficult for the mind to accommodate. Here I could clearly see that only in literature is there a continuity of images, only in literature does metaphor grow, amplify, elaborate, round itself off. Here, there was no continuity of images, I never saw any such thing; only discontinuity occurred. In a single instant, parallelism, metaphor, comparison were perceivable, then the gap grew, rapidly, spreading with insane rapidity from the tangential point.

9. F. Ludlow, *The Hasheesh Eater*, New York, 1857.

Dissociation[10] is the rule. Spontaneity consists of rebounds, ricochets, the return to unparallelism and divergence. It is only by a willed effort, for one's own gratification of a wish for consistency (which is a will to sequence), that in literature one image parallels another, to be followed by still others which all proceed in the same direction. Otherwise, they would not stay on parallel tracks but diverge with all speed. In three, four seconds, one is already far from one image to the next.

Another fact:
Another incomprehensible fact, and which has remained so: While I was listening, or trying to listen, to a lecture or somebody's speech on the radio—the speech of a government official, for instance—it happened repeatedly that with the speech a head would appear, perfectly simply and naturally, on the radio's woodwork, on one of the ornaments (a sort of shell) of the Louis XV paneling—never the same head, but a mildly animated head, its colors pastel or faded.

At times it was an entire small-sized bust, frequently in the costume of another age or another place. Neither the head, nor its expression, nor its attire or period gave any clear clue to a relation with the speaker, with his talk, with his character or his situation—not once.

Yet "my guest" on the wall made extended visits—sometimes lasting a good fifteen minutes or more. In the leaves of the trees in the courtyard I also saw, many times, many others, companions of the speeches and speech-makers; the reason for their presence and for my illusion never became clear. I did not have the excuse of speed as in the case of the interior visions, which passed with such dizzying motion;

10. The images, for their part, went their own way, not ours, and were of no help to me.

no, these visitors stayed quite still, making only slight gestures and faces. But not as if they were listening, either; rather like people who do not hear. Perhaps it is merely myself then, represented externally, myself vaguely annoyed, irritated? No, I would certainly have recognized something here or there in their expressions. And what about the costume of another age—not even considering the shapes of the heads, so very different from my own? Memories? A fusion of memories? But then, at least, I should have recognized one or the other. I should have penetrated some of the apparent meanings. I must behave as though this gathering, which has been there so many times, and different each time, did not exist. There is nothing I could say about it; I don't even know what to think about it.

There still remained an irritating discrepancy. These visitations had no purpose—that was my impression. But if it was a false impression? If, as is probable, there was some connection[11] anyway, how did this discrepancy, once I had found my partial explanation, remain so powerful, so persistent?

My error was to look, obstinately, for a connection, and above all a right connection.

11. One day when, all the same, a connection between the speaker and a type of uniform of fifty years ago seemed possible to me, might come to mind, it struck me that this thought had no effect on the image, the "visitor" installed on the woodwork. This connection perceived, he should have been wiped out for good, the illusion canceled, or, on the contrary, made more transparently and conventionally an illusion, its animation lost; but no, it remained undisturbed, continuing *to exist tranquilly*, unconcerned, untouched by my thoughts and pryings. If it had reappeared to me a number of times, I might have imagined, in this ancient mansion, that he was some spectral form of one of its occupants of long ago, whom I was permitted to see (at last a ghost); I might also have imagined being the witness of an earlier episode in the life of the person speaking. But none of this was really likely.

What is known of connections?[12] We are absolute beginners in such matters.

Every moment, it is true, is fraught with thousands of potential relations. In certain states of mind, neither the conscious nor the subconscious, both kept at a distance, is willing to establish connections that might be helpful to the person. In many regards, one has the impression of a nonpassive resistance inserted into the relations with the individual. One is tempted to speak of malice, clashes, noncollaboration, or alien interference.

The three categories cited here have been chosen because of the irritation produced by their appearance; yet, almost every thirty seconds something "unexplained" rushes by, lost as quickly as it is perceived; far from being able to guess its meaning, one could not even place its meaninglessness. Only by the gaps that are left does one know that they have been there.

12. One day (this was the first time I was ever present at such a sight) I saw a patient given shock treatment. She struggled, howled, though her screams were half smothered, against the terrifying, the supremely repulsive. I was deeply disturbed by this.

Questioned some minutes later by the psychiatrist, who had not flinched, she said that everything had been all right. What? In my turn, I questioned her. That panic, that horror in her face, in her gestures, in her whole attitude—what then was this drama she had experienced (or re-experienced)?

To every question she answered negatively, saying that it had been a pleasant experience.

Surely our memory, more so even than our immediate perception, is sometimes a break in associations, a wiping out of links, a reversal of relations, a wholesale canceling, the start of a renewal.

IX. THE FOUR WORLDS

Throughout these pages, much has been said of alienation, which in fact manifests itself as soon as one has absorbed certain substances that lead to madness, but may also lead to something entirely different.

How to behave, how to direct this surge of forces, of impulses, of desires, this fury, this explosive future?

Perhaps it is worth the trouble, for someone who has put himself in this infernal situation,[1] to know that the same disorganizing flux, the same frenzied surge which overflows in every direction, which cannot be controlled, retained, or contained, this same disorganizing force may become, for someone who knows how to deal with it, the very springboard of transcendence.

In ordinary life, the good and the bad—what is good for oneself, what is bad for oneself—are so intermingled, so linked, that often one gives up making a distinction.

In the state in question here, under the effect of these

1. During great disturbances, due to strong doses of neurodysleptics.

155

singularizing products, it is an entirely different matter; good exists entirely apart. What is "good" for oneself is perfectly different from what is "bad." The effects are immediate.

It is impossible to shilly-shally, to hesitate, to take a little of this, a little of that, neatly to balance between the two.

If it is good, it is good beyond all else, utterly exalting. If it is bad, it is terribly, unbearably bad, noxious, malevolent.

Nothing can be done by halves.

One risks one's mind by taking the wrong path. For every destination opens onto entirety.

In ordinary life, one passes harmlessly from the good to the very good, to the not so good, to the non-good. One is open to distractions, many distractions. By contrast, in this new state, when you are seized by dislocation, oppositions, effervescences, incoherence, and finally that madness which is uncontrollable fear, when you are carried away by the giant dragon, when it is no longer a question of pleasures, surprises, or even discoveries, then what is to be done? What is to be done when you have been outdistanced?

Well, there is one possible way to abort madness, to win it over during the very moments you are subject to it, undermined by it; there exists a possibility of transforming the scattering, dissipating, dislocating, devastating, breaking, tearing, disco-ordinating convulsiveness into an ally, into the prop, the support of radiance and illumination.[2]

---

2. Those who take drugs in order to surrender themselves to collective release and emotional abandon need not read further. There is nothing here that is meant for them. We do not speak the same language. We do not look for the same effects. He who is incapable of keeping his actions under control, incapable of confining everything to the *mind*, has missed the point completely.

The observer of psychic occurrences has to be "entrenched."

The absolute non-unity, the actual chaos, may, in just a few seconds, become erased and reversed, as a minus sign changes into a plus sign.

Not by returning to normality, utterly out of reach, unrealizable to even the slightest degree or extent, but by creating a super, monstrous, magnificent unity, as excessive as the dislocation of some seconds ago.

Unifying the minor currents which seem divergent but which secretly yearned for convergence, your divided realm will find itself in a unity, in a splendor of such unity that if someone had foretold it you would have declared it absurd, impossible, inhuman. Yet it happened, there it is.

All the minor currents from before no longer exist, but collaborate in a dynamic and unique impulse, joined in an impelling stream which permits no retrospection; a world in movement which sweeps you away. There exist four worlds (outside the natural world and the world of alienation). Only one appears at a time. These worlds categorically exclude the normal world and themselves are mutually exclusive.

Each of them corresponds distinctly and uniquely with an area of your body, which is brought to another level of energy, and receives a replenishment, a rejuvenation, and an instantaneous rekindling.

Some people must have discovered the first of these worlds by instinct during one of those critical, crucial moments, when you see no way to extricate yourself from a threatening situation. A great many more have found and perverted it at the same time, seeking to obtain from this very special world a gratification which it obviously offers (or perhaps also because they introduce into it language, scandalous actions, provocations, violence, which undo its unitary character). This is the world of pure eroticism.

Some, as we said, have discovered it; a smaller number have understood that one must remain within it *as it is*.

At once this world is redemptive. Being one, it closes the door to all which is not itself, and which ceases to appear; one, of a marvelously enveloping unity, not static, but circulating, so filled and fulfilling that a return to the habitual world no longer seems possible. It has become inconceivable, out of reach to the mind. You are committed to this solitary world, which reshapes itself, constantly restructures and fulfills itself in an extraordinary fashion.[3] Fear, the fear you have just left behind, however powerful and panic-striking it might have been, is instantaneously, totally wiped away. And for the entire time this enclave of extraordinary pleasure lasts (which is also a suspension of time, hence not accessible to the average man), throughout this time, which may be long, no idea, no image, however indifferent or alien, will recur—not even for the hundredth of a split second—without having become totally stripped of its sense, its meaning transformed, and unimaginable, not even by way of comparison. A universe without opposites, without contrast. You are redeemed. Saved from madness and liberated from the ordinary world, from the world where there is everything, from the world of diversity.

Currents of convergence now sustain you; no need for you to intervene. After a certain point, it is no longer your concern. The die is cast.

If the abstraction of the habitual world and the totalitarian onset of this erotic world occur a second time, on another day, it will readily be noted that this world is linked to the presence of a new force in the spinal column, inside

3. Cf. my *L'Infini turbulent*, chapter IV, *Mercure de France*, 1956.

one of the sacral vertebrae, a power which nourishes your extraordinary state, from which a continuous flux proceeds. Whatever the intensity of the sexual excitement, it is this area, replenished with new strength, which, although hidden, is master, on which everything depends; it is the dynamic nucleus which holds in check any tendency toward fear or any impression other than the erotic.

Nevertheless, a problem will arise; needless to say, it is nearly always improperly solved, solved in facility. Which is not a disaster and will even manifest an unusual radiance; and the fear will not return, or at least not at once. But one has bypassed something even more important.

If, having experienced this state once or more than once, one resists at the same point—the intimation of a stage where one remains arrested—vaguely feeling that there is something better to do, and that one can leave this erotic world for another level and yet not re-experience the separating and dislocating world of madness, only a person thus abandoning the security of eroticism may find what ought to be found.

So, at the last, or rather at the penultimate moment,[4] detaching himself from the erotic world, he leaves the intensified zone[5] to which this world has its physiological links. But to go where? If he finds no answer, he falls back into pulverizing and atomizing madness.

There remain three other worlds, into which the overstrained psychism may enter, all three completely exclusive, independent, full, closed. Only impulse, frenzied interior impulse, gains access to them and permits one to remain there.

How to enter one of them?

4. Inhibiting the impending orgasm and relief.
5. Intensified by the vertebra mentioned, the sacral center.

May it come, the magic word, sound, image which will discover for you this world within which you will be invulnerable!

May it come quickly!

For the search must not last long, otherwise you fall back into anguish, chaotic excitation, unbearable tension.

Chance may play its part, and a world you never suspected could hold you is revealed, taking you in willingly, more than willingly, rapturously. Something has released it and simultaneously, or a second before, has released the new state in which you are unrecognizable, an unprecedented outburst of valor swelling your chest and your entire being transfigured, become a dynamo of courage, ready for anything, eager to confront any risk.

Central and exorbitant.

Having reached this point, again there is no longer any room for fear. Agitations of all kinds, even if there was time for them to recur, disappear as though by magic. Fear is conjured away. You are in the realm of anti-fear. The basis and attraction of this anti-fear are intrepidity, valor, ardor, generosity, and gallantry, mysteriously, instantaneously rekindled, intensified, and everything that goes with disinterested impulse, sacrifice, self-confidence. The secret path through madness is self-surrender.

An exaltation which excludes all others. And all reason.

Just as previously, in the exceptional world of total eroticism, sadism was or might have been absent (it was uncalled for, since sensualization, in its unsurpassable fulfillment, was sufficient to itself, needing no stimulus), here too, in the world of heroism there is no hatred, vengeance, aggression, perversity, cruelty—the exaltation derives mainly from the idea of sacrifice. One has "heart."[6]

6. In the old sense of the word, as men used it.

But it is not in the heart that one experiences this world. The area in which one is now situated, from which one receives impulses and enrichment and new incessant replenishment, is also in the spinal column, but higher, at the waist.

Doubtless the impulse is forward, and impels forward. But the reservoir of strength which feeds it is behind, inside a lumbar vertebra which at this moment could be pointed to with the greatest precision.

This nucleus of strength imposes itself, hesitation is out of the question. It has been reached at great price. As you leave the erotic world for a world of valor, as you abandon the first for the second, the shock is tremendous. Particularly as you leave the first you experience a wrenching, so utterly unfamiliar that it leaves you breathless for a long time, in the certain expectation of an extraordinary, probably disastrous, and perhaps fatal phenomenon. The infidelity to the erotic center of the psyche, the wrenching from this magnificently reinforced, secure place where you had been magically arrested, from this nest of productive and continuous reinforcements, constitute an unprecedented dislocation which jars you deeply, to your very "vitals."

As though some occult law had been transgressed, you are left breathless, and your heart is like that of a horse which has taken a hurdle too high for it and can then no longer jump. But you have jumped . . . then everything starts up again. You wonder if this is not what the Kundalini's awakening would be like, the serpent power which must waken and "pierce" the higher centers or, rather, revive them. That is what it is like. So far, at least. You may have brushed past dangers. There has been a great shock.

In any case, you have been aroused, in an unprecedented fashion, from that nest which harbors whatever causes a person to be erotic and eroticized and, at the moment of yielding to its very temptation (which would have imprisoned you in it), you have revived your energy, raised it the length of the spinal column, there where it now sustains battles and everything else that emanates from and is adjacent to it, the site of an energy which now fills and prodigiously saturates you. You are no longer in the erotic world. Nothing is left of it but strength. No effort is called for. There is no longer any choice: the fighting spirit is given you as a grace. A prodigious phenomenon. You are still without hatred, wild with enthusiasm, cleansed of all cowardice, all vileness, all reserve and caution. Battle, a marvelous antidote against fear, released a fighting spirit free of anger, having no need of anger or any kind of animosity or rancor; you are in battle like a fish in water, or like fire in logs; devouring, insatiable, at home. You have aroused a second center.

There exist two more "beyonds," just as exclusive and closed, which are entered only by way of a sort of hurricane, and only to reach a world which is itself a hurricane, but the eye of a hurricane, where it is possible to live, and which is supremely Life itself. Access is gained by a transport, a trance. And such transports, such "abandoned" impulses, are possible only if the object is fathomless, if you can be sure that there is no need to be measured, cautious, informed, experienced.

It is the world of unbridled, sovereign love—yes, but above all of a transport of love.

The profane is represented by plurality, variety, which are caricatured by alienating excitation in a state of chaos and incoherence. The profane is not vileness, nor evil, but distraction, whose converse is meditation, a meditation, moreover, which without intensity is inoperative; in order to reach another level of energy, a *summum*, you have to operate the second or, rather, the tenth degree of intensity.

Gone are all separations, all divisions. Nothing distracts any more; distraction, with its continuously reductive concomitant, is the anti-sacred, even more than defilement.

An absolute exclusion sustains this galvanized state, the transport. How otherwise account for the non-profane character of the erotic world and that of valor? The same is true of this world of love, so different from that of eroticism, and yet only its transcendence, its miraculous transcendence. Once in this world, the merest hint of an impulse of love seems enough to immerse you suddenly in its impetuous current, in that tidal wave of love which utterly possesses you, utterly draws you in.

To hear many people speak, love would appear to be their sole occupation, their only haven. Yet, in disaster, it often fails the very ones who used to call on its name incessantly. This love presupposes a self-surrender so absolute that such people would have no conception of it, would indeed give it a wide berth, perhaps not even suspecting its existence.

Here, once taken under this wing, your opinion no longer counts; what you think you thought instantly becomes the past, is superseded; you are seized, taken up, carried away. No more prejudices, no more preferences, no more principles. No more judgments. Choice, manner, outcome no longer concern you. This world is given to you, and with the gift you move toward ever more gifts, an infinity of gifts.

To experience such love means to know how to let yourself be borne.

The virtue to maintain here, therefore, is a certain quality of hope; it is in response to this that grace answers—in response to an invisible, effective, humble, unconquerable, undemonstrative hope, perhaps unknown to its possessor.

How and why does one enter this world?

Once the tendency to hatred is driven hence, the delights of loving, of being able to love, are overwhelmingly present.

An all-conquering attraction, an omnipresent attraction. All resistance stops.

It is the perfect anxiety-free celebration, the celebration of love. A mystery that is celebrated in the most psychically naked way.[7] The Immense is there, but not maddening. It suits you and you It. You adapt to it, your heart slaked and at the same time unsatiated. There is no need to be on your guard, to take precautions. No discord. Harmony itself.

Plenitude. Infinity unmitigated. Infinity. Without reserve, without withdrawal, without distance.

One has put oneself in the right current.

Fear, ousted and annulled, like a stranger about whom nothing is known, has lost its very meaning.

One is filled with energy, radical energy, for energy surpasses, if possible, even beatitude and psychic felicity (an

---

7. Love has many different ways. Thus the love of the divine, as religions demonstrate, is sometimes a propensity to celebrate, at other times to humble oneself in its presence, or a propensity to blind submission, to sacrifice or awe, or unification. In other contexts it may be a tendency following the model of a loving child's relation to his father, of the relations between a betrothed couple, or that of the lover to his mistress. Each may lend its structure to transcendence. Prayer and supplication are mainly an appeal; here appeal and answer are simultaneous in fulfillment, experienced as immediate plenitude.

The believer, the "servant" of a cult dedicated to a personalized God, will move toward Him.

Whereas for someone who conceives of an immanent God, love is an expansion in every direction, meeting Infinity on all sides and in an inexpressible joy.

The astonishing thing is that one cannot approach Infinity without felicity.

energy that supplants all lesser impulses), a vast, torrential, supreme energy.[8]

Ecstasy, no, *enstasy*. One doesn't have to see angels; one undergoes a transforming irradiation.

The state of exalted eroticism, exalted fearlessness, exalted love, exalted contemplation—of these four states, who could fail to desire the last above all others?

Yet he who expected to be at home there does not reach it.

One cannot gain a footing in this territory in a natural fashion. The attitude of abandon is indispensable. Experts in religion, subjected to the influence of these expansion-generating substances, squirmed and fidgeted like irreverent children.[9] Others merely remained outside, unable to enter.

Even when prepared by meditation, some felt that they were lost and going mad; or, merely tormented, they sulked, became furious. Who can tell if he is prepared? If despite or because of a science of concentration, he is not actually unprepared?

One expert[10] in mental discipline, initiated into the

8. The fusing point or location of extreme pressure, which in the body corresponds to sanctifying love, is inside one of the vertebrae situated higher on the spinal column, at the level of the diaphragm.

9. R. C. Zaehner, Professor of Eastern Religions at Oxford: *Mysticism: Sacred and Profane*, 1967.

10. John Blofeld, in "Yogic Experience with Mescaline," *Psychedelic Review*, no. 7, 1966: "My fear of permanent madness increased and I suffered especially from the feeling of having no inner self or center of consciousness into which to retreat from the tension and to take rest."

This expert's confession will indirectly explain and, if need be, excuse those who, anticipating the insensate explosion of images and ideas, incoherence and raging chaos, and finding no stability, have resorted to the equilibrating sexual center, after which they were able to elevate themselves. Although being able practices of Eastern meditation and Zen, remained lost completely for a long time, unable to find a *center*.

When he finally reached it, "it was through renunciation." And it is not easy to abandon oneself, even knowing that this is what is called for. Fear still amounts to a struggle, is the painful representation of a resistance . . . an unhappy one.

Whichever path one takes, that is, whether one reaches this state directly, by natural inclination, or by passing first through the center situated lower down, but which is also stronger—once there, it is like lightning on a dark night, all illumination, but it is a lightning that lasts. What has preceded is forgotten.

This, surely, is where the surge of unifiers had to lead, to Unity itself.

Unsought-for. The invasion of Unity has been accomplished without you, apparently without needing your convictions, a promethean operation, in an expanded consciousness.

Bliss by depersonalization.

If expansiveness is one of the characteristics of the divine, tension is much more so.

There are better things to do than oppose currents.

The dissociated, incoherent, and disruptive may have been a necessary impetus to its opposite, its exalted opposite. These turmoils, having become *one* transport, have reached their necessary destination.

---

to do without it is assuredly best for the majority. The starting point is important. This is manifest in Tantric texts. Liberating as they are, they are at the root of the tree. Yet once the energy of the erotic center is transferred to a superior center, *not a single erotic image or idea returns.* Only the forces of this center, not its images and its world pass on to a higher level.

No more happenings. No more episodes, calculations—no more plurality.[11]

No more duality. Most strangely, it is ended; only after having recovered somewhat from the exalted state, is one able to realize the extreme strangeness of this.

Suddenly, duality no longer exists. Deliverance.

The insignificance of the mind's constructions stands revealed.

Pure contemplation. One no longer thinks in terms of qualities, designations, definitions, one does without them; a wind has passed overhead, a psychic wind which annuls the definitions, the categories before they are born.

Illumination: a radically non-appropriating contemplation, which only receives, absolutely non-conquering, absolutely tranquilizing, de-egoizing, blinding the minor discriminations[12] in favor of a huge unprecedented insight.

The intelligence of distinctions finds itself stupefyingly supplanted.

The spirit of evaluation is totally gone. Interest is disinterested. But the countless variety of the world must still be somewhere . . . It is there only if one tries to seize, to classify, to delimit, to define.

One is beyond, now.

Within a non-profane, non-utilitarian wisdom.

The absolute: true non-violence.

11. It is difficult to watch the stream of colors and sounds go by and to take in impressions without classifying them, without somehow relying on this delimitation, where the one is observed and the other an observer, where the subject is on one side, the object on the other, and objects have their place in space, and their purpose. It seems impossible to go against it. Yet here one does it, without even trying.

12. That is, one nearly always lets them pass, without establishing any relation to them. In fact, relations subsist, but spectacularly reduced, which radically transforms the over-all impression.

Comments

Anyone who has not been shaken to the core will not get there, though he may often be on the verge of getting there . . . If only he didn't cling to this or that definition, or to some distracting thought. Also, the very idea of abandoning oneself utterly to another world must be disturbing to most people, so that they avoid it instinctively, without even realizing it.

The centers:
What a leap is required to pass from one to the other, particularly from the first (the lower) to the higher ones!
For it is a question of relinquishing the center of eroticism at its maximum tension, to put to mental or psychic use a phenomenon at its point of consummation, in resistance to physical pleasure. A memorable transition. A tour de force or an audacity—and since one has the feeling of having violated a law of nature, one wonders what will come of it, if life will follow . . .

As a rule, considerable drawbacks will lead to abandoning these experiments.

Along with absorption into the world of eroticism, one experiences a *concentration of energy* in the sacral vertebrae. To the world of exalted valor corresponds a concentration in the lumbar vertebrae. The world of supranatural attraction and irresistible love is associated with a concentration in the dorsal vertebrae. As for illuminative contemplation, this constitutes an arc which extends from a cervical vertebra to various points of the encephalon. It does not follow that *centers* are involved, and still less, anatomically distinguishable centers. Rather, it is a question of relay points, preferred transitions for exceptional circumstances.

It is not for me to say whether or not these are chakras. It must be remembered[1] that the chakras are not identified with the navel, the solar plexus, the throat, and other areas on the front of the body, as pictorial representations indicate, but much more (though not precisely identified but merely associated) with certain subtle medullary centers which correspond to them.

Despite impulses which as such, it would seem, ought to move forward or upward, or in the direction of the heart or the genitals, I always felt pulled down, pulled back (in each of the nests or reinforced centers of the marrow) and radiating from there.

Impurity may be a hindrance. The ascent, the repeated ascent, for example, from the center in a sacral vertebra to a cervical center surely is not natural.

After a first experiment with this eroticizing center, one may on another occasion and, seemingly immediately (that is, without having to pass through that center again),

1. Arthur Avanlon, *The Serpent Power.*

achieve the transition to the cervical center that corresponds to illumination.

It would be a mistake to suppose that, knowing the paths, one will regain them; that having known worlds of ecstasy, one will be able to return to them at will. Not at all. Will is of no account, nor conscious desire. It is in one's deep unconscious, where one cannot know what presently exists, that everything first happens, it is from there that a world of jubilation will emerge . . . provided a certain genuine aspiration is on the alert.
Terror may also come, it is a frequent occurrence; terror is always, and particularly in the chaos of the moment, a favored possibility.

But, someone will say, aren't these worlds without object, beyond an object, love without object, contemplation without object—aren't such worlds so much smoke, leaving behind even less than smoke?
A new expanse, a profoundly hollowed depth, which may afterward be partially filled, but not annulled, subsists after the experiment and perhaps forever, though not quite uniformly either.

These rare states, such as the sojourns in these four worlds, have become possible because of an abandonment, an acceptance, a yea-saying.
Now each man is a "yes" with certain "no's." After the unprecedented and somewhat counter-natural acceptances, one must expect recurrences of such refusals; however, there is a part that cannot be erased or reversed, which continues to function, living on the margins of the Unforgettable.

Evolution in process . . .